ART DIRECTION
FOR
FILM AND VIDEO

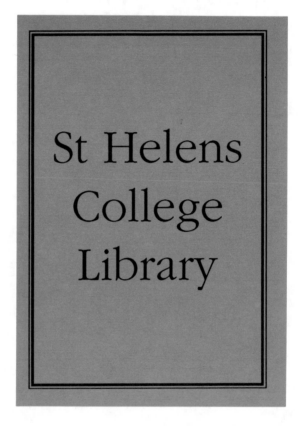

ART DIRECTION FOR FILM AND VIDEO

Robert Olson

Focal Press
Boston London

Many products are claimed as trademarks. Where this occurs, and Butterworth–Heinemann is aware of a trademark claim, the trademark is acknowledged with initial capital letters (e.g. Pink Pearl).

Focal Press in an imprint of Butterworth–Heinemann.

Copyright © 1993 by Butterworth–Heinemann
ℝ A member of the Reed Elsevier group
All rights reserved.

Drawings and photographs by Robert Olson

Recognizing the importance of preserving what has been written, it is the policy of ♾ Butterworth–Heinemann to have the books it publishes printed on acid-free paper, and we exert our best efforts to that end.

Library of Congress Cataloging-in-Publication Data

Olson, Robert.
   Art direction for film and video / by Robert Olson.
      p.   cm.
   Includes index.
   ISBN 0-240-80189-X (alk. paper)
      1. Motion pictures—Art direction.   2. Motion pictures—Setting and scenery.   3. Television—Stage-setting and scenery.   I. Title.
PN1995.9.A74048 1993
791.43'025—dc20   93-28799
                                                                         CIP

British Library Cataloguing-in-Publication Data
A catalogue record for this book is available from the British Library.

Butterworth–Heinemann
80 Montvale Avenue
Stoneham, MA 02180

10 9 8 7 6 5 4 3 2 1

†ed in the United States of America

Dedicated to
Gabor Kalman,
a friend indeed

CONTENTS

PREFACE

WHAT'S IN THIS BOOK

This book details the thinking and basic drawing techniques art directors and production designers need and follows the progress of typical projects from script analysis to setup on stage and location. While other helpful books are available that communicate techniques, this book, based on the work experience of a film and video art director, relates technique to everyday work experiences every art director encounters.

WHO CAN BENEFIT FROM THIS BOOK?

Film students can make their projects more professional looking by knowing how to ask for help realistically with location and set projects. Producers, directors, and writers can see how an efficient art director can work with them more effectively. Designers such as graphic artists, advertising art directors, layout artists, and painters and sculptors can learn how to adapt their design skills to film and video projects. Anyone considering a career in video and film art direction can see what the profession is really like.

ABOUT THE AUTHOR

The author has worked as art director and set designer at the major motion picture and television facilities in Los Angeles, as well as freelancing for many corporate, entertainment, and cable television producers. Along with professional work, the author created and taught a continuing art direction curriculum for UCLA Extension, including several one-day design seminars presenting top Hollywood production designers. Other seminars include a weeklong course for the Televisa Mexico design staff in Mexico City, Stanford University Summer Workshop, and courses at Art Center College of Design in Pasadena, California.

ACKNOWLEDGMENTS

The author wishes to thank the producers and directors who have provided a creative working atmosphere, the staff at UCLA Extension who made it possible to meet so many talented and motivated students, and particularly Karen Speerstra and Sharon Falter at Focal Press, who have made the publication of this book possible, for their invaluable guidance.

INTRODUCTION

This book is for anyone who wants to learn about production design, whether they are students, producers, directors, writers, or designers who want to work in the film and television industries. The information is presented in easy-to-understand practical terms, emphasizing an imaginative approach to everyday situations.

Due to the wide-ranging nature of this book, the information is divided into three parts: "The Role and Responsibilities of a Production Designer," "Outline of a Job," and "Typical Sets and Opportunities."

Part I illustrates where production designers came from, what a production designer is and does, the basic materials and tools used by designers, and a sample project showing different approaches to lighting a set after it is designed and built.

Part II tracks a dramatic series pilot from script to wrap-up. By following the detailed illustrated instructions, a beginner can learn to analyze the script, research the characters' environments, work effectively with the producer and director, produce sketches and construction drawings, make a model, and supervise the construction, setup, and decoration of the set.

Part III details several typical design challenges met in professional work situations: a series pilot shot on location, a talk show, a news broadcasting environment, and a film commercial. The last chapter tells the beginner how to prepare a portfolio and résumé and how to look for work in the film and broadcasting industries.

THE ROLE AND RESPONSIBILITIES OF THE PRODUCTION DESIGNER

To understand the origin and development of production design, we will first see how the increasing popularity and improving technology of motion pictures required better stories and acting, as well as more-believable settings. Many designers came from the theater, along with theatrical setting techniques, but as the film industry developed, designers created design and building techniques that satisfied the needs of the new film medium.

Part I describes the production designer's responsibilities, basic set elements, the production environment in which the designer works, and illustrates lighting techniques that affect the designer's work.

WHAT IS A PRODUCTION DESIGNER?

A production designer develops a visual plan for an entire production, including sets, props, costumes, color schemes, lighting, and frequently the entire flow of a film. As film is a visual medium, the "look" the production designer establishes can involve the audiences emotionally as much as story lines and dialogue. Effective production design can translate a popular two-dimensional newspaper cartoon character such as Popeye or Dick Tracy into costumed live actors and three-dimensional environments that give the flavor of the original cartoon strips.

Production design has a strong history in films. As the popularity of special effects films escalates, the respect awarded production designers, whose imaginations create fantasy worlds inhabited by heretofore unimagined characters, increases as well. In some productions, a production designer can have as much authority as the director.

WHAT DOES A PRODUCTION DESIGNER DO?

The production designer makes a thorough study of the script, does research, and confers with the producer and director to develop the "look" and flow of color and form from one sequence to the next.

A production designer is usually retained for the duration of a film. Sometimes producers hire the designer to create a general design scheme and mood and the designer—after providing them with detailed information on the design plan for the film—turns the project over to a staff of art directors and set designers.

THE PRODUCTION DESIGNER'S STAFF

Once the production designer creates a general scheme for a film, a staff of designers helps the production designer develop the scheme. One or more art directors supervise the design, drafting, and production of the sets and locations. An illustrator or visualizer develops picture compositions and continuity. The costume designer creates costumes that complement the look delineated by the production designer. Experts working with smoke, water, explosives, lasers, and computers; matte painters; and model makers contribute their skills to the production design staff.

Where Did Production Designers Come From?

David O. Selznick first officially bestowed the title on William Cameron Menzies in 1939 for his contributions to *Gone with the Wind*, which included the direction of some sequences. Before that, art directors were responsible for everything that didn't move, but didn't have the comprehensive visual authority of today's production designer. To understand how the profession of art direction and production design evolved, let's start with the early development of the film medium.

PICTURES BEGIN TO MOVE

Scholars can argue endlessly about when motion pictures were first invented, in which country, and by whom. We know that in 1888 the Thomas Edison Laboratory demonstrated a primitive motion picture device that was the forerunner of a revolution in popular entertainment.

Not many people paid much attention to motion pictures at first, as they were regarded as a fascinating novelty that would remain just that. When movies got longer, though, the public went for them in a big way. People would pay a nickel to watch anything that moved on the flickering screens of rented halls.

The Audience Increases

The novelty of simple movement wore off before long, however, and motion picture producers saw that they would have to manufacture longer and better films. They turned to the most obvious source of material: the theater. With the actors and plays came theatrical sets and backdrops and a lot of theatrical tradition, which still exists in the motion picture business.

Motion pictures were made outdoors to take advantage of free sunlight. No one had thought of using electric light to light the sets and actors. Some producers perched cameras and sets on rooftops where tall buildings could not block the sunlight. They hoped the wind would not be strong enough to cause the rented, theatrically painted drawing room wall to flap or the dining room tablecloth to wave unconvincingly during a dinner party scene. The audience would end up laughing in the wrong places. Wind, rain, snow, and ice could seriously halt production and deprive the clamoring audiences of their amusement and the producer of cash. Producers moved inside buildings with glass roofs or skylights, which solved their problems with the elements for a while. If they didn't want to hire a set designer, producers would round up some local carpenters and have them build realistic rooms, just as the carpenters did when they built real houses. The exterior shots were done wherever they could grab them. It became apparent, however, that the talents of set designers were needed, as sets built by house carpenters and decorated by the producer's sister did not look right when translated to film. The sets had to be designed and built to meet the demands of the camera eye.

Movie Makers Move On

Producers ground film through their cameras, processed and edited it, and rushed it out to any exhibitor who paid the rental fee. Due to some unpleasantness over camera mechanism patents, producers moved south and west to distance themselves from the patent law enforcers and to enjoy more shooting days per year than the weather allowed in the Northeast. Florida, Arizona, and the San Francisco Bay area had thriving film studios, but the variety of terrain and pleasant weather in Southern California attracted the major part of the growing film industry. An added attraction was the proximity of the Mexican border, which allowed producers to throw their clandestine cameras in a car and to speed across the border to safety, leaving the process servers hired by the camera mechanism cartel on the other side of the border.

Versions of Paris

Movie moguls discovered that once they owned a piece of land, they could build their own two-dimensional plaster-and-chicken-wire cities, western towns, and hillsides. The lot system also gave producers some control over the weather. Many studio back-lot streets included cables stretched over the streets that could support opaque canvas covers to provide shelter from unwanted rain and could help simulate night darkness during the day. Overhead perforated pipes could spray rain, which might fall gently or be whipped into hurricane force by motor-driven fans. Some studios constructed dump tanks, into which portions of ships were placed to be deluged with tons of water during sea storm sequences.

The Studio Production Line

The studios became film factories, turning out features and short films on a production-line basis. During the 1930s MGM made a feature film a week and had over two thousand employees on its regular payroll. Studios recruited designers from the New York theatrical world as well as from Europe. They designed and built portions of cities on Hollywood lots and in the barnlike stages that rose like housing projects. If a picture needed a French drawing room, the set would be built on a stage and dressed with the appropriate furniture and drapery. A later film might use the same walls dressed as a New York City townhouse or a country place.

The lot system delighted producers. Their desire was to keep the major portion of production right under their noses so they could watch what was going on. Studios kept dozens of actors under contract and assigned them to emote in one picture after another. Each major studio had its version of the cities of the world. Many of the directors, as well as the art directors, were from Europe, so the flavor of the back-lot architecture varied according to the nationality of its designers.

WORK IN THE MOVIES? NEVER!

At first, theatrical designers looked down their noses at the vulgarity of movies, but many changed their attitude as the quality of films improved and the creative possibilities became apparent. Architects began to put their skills to work in the film industry. Here was a chance to put their imagination to work on never-never lands of plaster and fantasy. They could say good-bye to dull apartment houses and office buildings and live in the magical world of motion pictures. Many art directors were recruited from architectural schools. Studios lured designers from the theater and put them to work on musicals. The architects worked on films that required the reproduction of buildings. They had to adjust to working with surfaces rather than internal structure; after all, their work only had to last until the picture was finished, not for the ages. They designed portions of buildings, the parts to be seen by the camera, and trained their eyes to see as the camera sees.

Art Directors Become Stars

As the major studios grew, they employed many art directors. A supervising art director guided the art department staff of designers and developed a visual style for the studio, much as today's production designers design a look for an individual film. MGM's Cedric Gibbons was surely one of the most colorful and influential motion picture supervising art directors. Some say that Mr. Gibbons never picked up a pencil, while others claim to have seen him laboring over architectural detailing. He created the Big White Set look for Metro by adapting the Art Deco movement's ideas to Metro film design.

While many individual art directors made notable contributions to the visual style of motion pictures made by major Hollywood studios, the following people stand out as stylistic innovators.

WILFRED BUCKLAND—New York stage designer
Brought to Hollywood by Cecil B. DeMille
1915—Championed artificial lighting

VAN NEST POLGLASE—RKO supervising art director
Studied architecture and interior design
Designed Art Deco Astaire musicals
Worked at other studios as well as at RKO

RICHARD DAY—Freelance
Self-taught Canadian
Worked primarily at Fox
Designed many Erich Von Stroheim films

WILLIAM CAMERON MENZIES—Freelance
Studied at Art Students League
Worked as an advertising artist
Directed some sequences of *Gone with the Wind*
Awarded first production designer credit

TELEVISION CHANGES THE FILM BUSINESS

The United States saw its first public exhibition of television in 1927, but it wasn't until after World War II that TV became as universally fascinating as motion pictures were at their infancy. Television receivers progressed from huge revolving disks and forests of wires and tubes behind tiny, blurry screens to acceptable pieces of furniture that dominate America's living rooms. Seeing this trend, and alarmed at the way people stayed at home in the evening watching free TV, the motion picture studios developed wide-screen processes, enhanced sound systems, and epic films to keep their the-ater audiences, and just to be on the safe side, produced programs for television as well.

Just as theater designers had been reluctant to work in the film medium when it first started, many motion picture art directors did not want to work in television. The budgets were low, production time was limited, and prestige was low.

Make Way for the Sitcoms

The major studios jumped on the television bandwagon. Large studios had all the facilities for making pictures and used them to feed television's growing appetite. Staff art directors who were accustomed to big budgets and plenty of time were now assigned to television series that had neither. The big outdoor sets were used, as well as the standing sets on studio stages. Sometimes television series used sets that had been built for feature pictures not released until long after the set had been seen on television.

Whole series and episodes were written to use existing sets. Studios that were accustomed to finishing a picture a month now found themselves pushed into producing what amounted to a picture a week for television series.

Film to Tape Transfer

Videotape recording changed television practices and programming. Now it was possible to record television images instantaneously, edit them, and produce a program in a fraction of the time it took to create a program on film, which required laboratory processing. Picture quality improved along with the speed of production. In the same way that filmmaking equipment became smaller and more portable, video equipment did the same. Today's video cameras weigh less than twenty-five pounds and produce broadcast-quality images. Editors no longer have to cut tape with a razor blade and splice it together. The editing is done electronically.

Improved Technology Affects Art Directors

In its infancy, television equipment was very demanding. Art directors had to work with a limited range of gray values, and had to avoid extreme contrasts of value as well as certain patterns. The old camera tubes could retain an image if held on the same picture too long. The system required high, even light levels, which limited the amount of contrast and atmosphere an art director could present. Technicolor, the first generally used color film system in the United States, by contract required the services of a color consultant, who required art directors to work within limits set up by laboratory processing. Art directors had to work with a fairly limited color palette and saw their sets flooded with intense flat light, which limited the amount of mood and atmosphere they could create.

As television and film technology improved, art directors were freed from many of these limitations. They could begin using glitter, lights shining into the lens, and a more subtle color range. Many art directors began to specialize as the range of programming widened. Some freelance art directors set up design studios that specialized in situation comedies, or game shows, or news broadcasts. Film laboratories developed film stocks that did not come with rigid lab requirements, giving art directors more design freedom.

The Visual Future

The onward march of technology, including high-definition video and enhanced computer manipulation of images, will change the role of art directors. Virtual reality systems, which use two small color screens placed in a headset before our eyes, and work with a sensor-equipped bodysuit connected to a computer system, can place the viewer in a synthetically created environment.

Someone will create new visual worlds. Who better than art directors, who are experienced in dealing with images seen through lenses and imagination?

In the next chapter we will see what qualities art directors and production designers need to have, and later, how they put their talents and technical skills to work.

WHAT DOES
AN ART DIRECTOR
NEED TO KNOW?

Production designers and art directors are supposed to know a little bit about everything, but here are some areas about which they need to know a lot.

AN ART DIRECTOR SHOULD BE VISUALLY AWARE

The world around us is a feast of images: people, trees, houses, animals, buildings, clouds, and sunsets, all of which enhance our enjoyment of life as well as providing design ideas. When walking down the street, look at everything as design. That sign up there! What great colors, and look at the bank of traffic lights! Imagine it enlarged to twenty feet high with the lights pulsing to music. Down the street is a building being demolished. The floors are peeled away, revealing a four-story collage wall of decades of wallpaper and paint. It could be hanging in a museum.

Many art directors carry a pocket camera to record images like these. One art director was having difficulty finding the right color and texture for a newly discovered planet to be seen in a science-fiction series. She stepped out of her car one day, glanced down into the gutter, and saw a piece of refuse that was exactly right. She snapped a picture of it, had the photo image computer-wrapped around a sphere, and created the new planet, all because her eyes were open to everything.

YOU'RE IN DEMAND IF YOU CAN DRAW

Drawing is more than putting lines down on paper. It is learning to see. We have all heard "Why, I can't draw a straight line with a ruler!" The person who says this has abandoned all hope. If the art director is visually aware, the ability to draw is helpful, if not essential. Some production designers and art directors don't draw well. They have someone else do it. If the designer works at a major studio, the talents of sketch artists and visualizers are available. Their job is to communicate the art director's ideas visually in sketches and illustrations. They are wonderful people to have around, but if you're freelancing, it's creatively helpful, economical, and quicker to be able to make your own sketches. Also, during the process of making a sketch, ideas present themselves and can be worked into your plan immediately, which saves a lot of time. It's fun to see a brilliant idea creep over the top of your drawing board. If you can draw, you can capture it before it gets away.

ANOTHER DIMENSION

An understanding of three-dimensional form is an essential part of an art director's skills. How else can one put shapes together and have them work from more than one angle? Cameras shoot from many positions. While a set may look terrific from straight on, how will it look from other angles?

Making sculpture is an excellent way to learn to think in the round. While working with clay, metal, plastic, and other materials, the sculptor turns the piece to the eye, much as the camera roams about a set. The elements present can be seen from many different angles from setup to setup, when the actors are moving and reacting to each other. Situation comedy sets, however, are somewhat like theater sets in the sense that an audience is present and has a fixed, limited viewing angle, but the elements within the set need to present a three-dimensional aspect.

WHAT COLORS DO YOU LIKE?

Art directors need to know the physical theory of color and how it works. The human retina has 125 million receptors, called cones, that are sensitive to light-dark values of light, which the lens focuses upon them. The retina also has 7 million rods that perceive red, green, and blue. Our brains mix these values into what we know as colors. This type of color mixing of light is *additive mixing*. Television picture tubes are composed of rows of red, green, and blue dots also, which fluoresce in various combinations when struck by the cathode ray beam, producing what we see as thousands of different colors.

Paints, dyes, and inks, however, follow different rules. When white light falls on a yellow card, for example, the yellow pigment absorbs all colors except yellow, which is reflected, making our eyes perceive the color yellow. This system is called the *subtractive* system, as colors are absorbed.

The description of colors is a subjective process, so to provide an objective view, art directors provide color chips and color sketches for scenic artists and set painters. Production designers use color for psychological and stylistic effect by keying certain colors to characters, scenes, and sequences. Some designers work out the general color progression from scene to scene before they do any other, more specific, design scheme. If a character's personality is villainous, the designer may use a lot of black, or if the character is a happy type, the color may be yellow or pink.

DRAFTING

Production designers and art directors need ways to communicate visual ideas. Construction drawings provide detailed information on set construction, as you will see later. Film and television drafting differs from other types because it deals more with surfaces than with internal structure. Architects and engineers are more concerned with the mechanics and engineering of buildings and mechanical devices. Many art directors do not do their own drafting. They have studio draftspeople available or can hire assistants to do the construction drawings.

MATERIALS

To design a set, an art director needs to know what the materials are and what they can do. What good is a set that cannot be built? Sets are commonly built on soundstages, but building plays a major role in location work, too. A building at a location may have the general qualities the production needs but may need alterations that must be designed and added to the structure. To save time, sets that have no architectural relationship to the location buildings or landscape can be constructed within easy reach of the company while it is there at the location.

LIGHTING

As part of the process of designing a set, the art director needs to know the basics of lighting. Without light, the set will not be visible to the camera, and as sets should be presented in the best possible way, the art director should produce designs that don't create major problems for the lighting director. It isn't necessary to know how many ohms resistance are in how many feet of cable or how many lighting instruments one dimmer can handle. It's enough to know a few basic requirements, such as the following: an exterior backing should be hung about eight feet away from a window; large areas of shiny surface require extra time (money) and care to light; sets with ceilings can complicate the lighting process. It's a good idea to make the lighting director a friend. As you will see later, lighting can make your work look better than you had hoped, or it can destroy your many hours of hard work and enthusiasm.

HELPFUL PERSONAL QUALITIES

The art director needs to know how to work effectively with the other members of the company. The art director's staff needs clear supervision so that the result will have a cohesive look. The art director should find the best solution to each problem in an innovative way. How easy it is to dig out an old set of drawings and have a reverse print made that can be presented as a new solution. Every production has its own needs and requires a different set of solutions.

Flexibility Is a Plus

Designing a show is like assembling a collage. The pieces are loose and may have to be put together quickly under a new set of rules. Changes will be made over which the art director has no control. Be flexible. When the groaning and complaining are over, go ahead and work under the new rules. What if the director asks you to change the most beloved part of your design? First, state the reasons you designed the set the way you did. Second, be willing to consider the reasons the director gives for wanting the changes. If the reasons are valid, be willing to change your design. If the reasons do not make sense, diplomatically try to change the director's mind. If you cannot, change the set. After all, the director is the *director.*

Passengers! Try to Remain Calm!

Each production is different. When everyone is in a hurry, tempers flare and resentments build. Patient methodical attention to detail is a discipline that has to be practiced. Many times things go wrong at the last minute. The more foresight the art director can apply, the more will be available to take care of the unscheduled disasters. What if it rains? Is the cyclorama *really* flameproof? Will the ice sculpture for the party scene melt too soon?

What a Business

An art director needs to have an effective business sense. The popular assumption is that sensitive creative people like us can't balance our checkbooks without help. Some of us can't, but we have to keep track of where the money is going. Estimating costs and making up budgets is a vital part of the business. The art director deals with large amounts of money, at least on paper, and this money has to be parceled out to many suppliers, all of whom need to be kept happy. An example of a budget will be presented later.

It's OK to Be Disorganized Sometimes

When you're getting your ideas together is the best time for confusion. This is the time when you have some facts and ideas for your particular brand of creative process to grind up. Use as much paper as you need, and fearlessly fill up the wastebasket. Put down every idea that has possibilities. When you have settled down and regained your composure and the wastebasket is full of terrible ideas, pat yourself on the back for coming up with a brilliant solution and calmly set about bringing it to reality. *This* is the time to be organized. Many a good idea has become the object of scorn because the designer didn't take it apart and figure out how to build it. Remember that the solution is in the problem.

Wish You'd Stayed on the Farm or Majored in Accounting?

Nothing is going according to plan. The 120 gallons of specially mixed paint are the wrong color. Someone forgot to tell you that there will be twelve guests in the dinner party scene (the one with the melting ice sculpture) instead of six. The paint won't dry on the giant mushrooms and the elves are waiting to sit on them. The director has decided to shoot the biggest set a week earlier than announced. Things always work out somehow, and the show gets done. Don't be surprised if you have to help unstick the elves. After all, art directors are supposed to know a little bit about everything.

In the next chapter we will take a tour of the environment in which we will put all these qualities and skills to work.

THE PRODUCTION ENVIRONMENT

The television medium presents many challenges to the production designer. Whether the recording medium is film or tape, the designer needs to know how the systems work, how to cope with the limitations, and how to exploit the mediums' advantages. However, what the designer envisions and what the viewer at home sees may differ dramatically, even though the design team has carefully controlled the set elements placed on the stage or chosen on location. We will see in this chapter what basic physical elements the designers work with on the stage, how they work, and the picture limitations.

LINES AND DOTS

The amount of fine detail the video camera can show is more limited than the amount a film camera can show. The American system uses 525 lines of picture information, compared to most of European video, which shows 625 lines. Motion picture film contains millions of grains of picture information in each frame. A clumsily attached doorknob plate will be about two inches wide on the face of an average television screen, but can be eight feet in diameter on a thirty-foot-wide motion picture screen. Designers should never allow sloppy craftsmanship to slip by just because it's for TV but should demand the maximum quality time and budget allow. What if the director decides to use a very tight close-up of that badly fastened doorknob plate, even if it is only three inches wide? You thought nobody would notice.

Different Perceptions

A major variable is the adjustment of the picture seen by the home viewer. We have all had the experience of entering someone's living room when the television set is on and wondering how they could watch TV in those exaggerated colors. Individual color perceptions and tastes are unique, so the color mixture and level adjustment of the set may be very high and the contrast level may be very low. Picture quality can be highly distorted, compared to what it was when it left the broadcasting facility or cable system. Some viewers do not feel they are getting their money's worth if they do not see lots of color, so they increase the color saturation. Generally, colors show up brighter and more saturated on camera than they look to the eye. A guiding rule is to choose paint tones that are a step down in saturation from the color you want perceived on the tube or screen.

How Does the Video Picture Get from Here to There?

These are the main steps the picture goes through between the time the lens focuses the reflected light from your carefully designed setting and reassembles the image on a home screen.

1. Light reflected from an object is focused by the camera lens onto the face of the picture tube.
2. The picture tube translates the light, dark, and color variations into electronic information that is sent to the camera control equipment.
3. The images from cameras and other sources are mixed and recorded on magnetic tape (unless a live broadcast).
4. The electronic information is sent via cable or microwave transmission to a transmitter, where it is again manipulated and transformed into a signal that is broadcast. If the signal is relayed by satellite, the image can travel fifty thousand miles.
5. The image is picked up by the home antenna or is introduced by cable into the receiving set, where it is again translated into a viewable picture.

What the picture's odyssey means to the art director is that these variables must be kept in mind when designing sets.

Bold Is Best

Let's look at some wallpaper. When leafing through sample books, remember that your eyes are just a few inches away from the color and pattern. Walk across the store and look at the sample from a distance. Does the color read as a definite color, or does it turn into an indefinable gray? Does the pattern come across or does it become a mushy texture? When choosing colors, textures, and forms, choose the definite and direct, which tells its story at a glance.

Now that we have seen what some of the system's limitations are and how the picture gets from here to there, let's get acquainted with the environment in which our sets will stand.

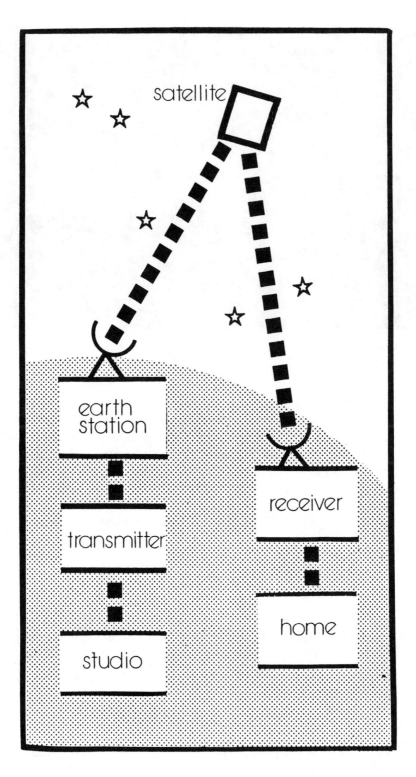

THE PRODUCTION STAGE

The physical home of a production is usually a barnlike building containing a lot of empty space. Stages come in many sizes, shapes, and locations, the choice of which depends on the production's needs. If the producer works on a lot with many stages, the production will be assigned an available stage. An independent producer will shop around for a stage that serves the production's needs and budget. Ideally, the producer will consult the art director before the stage space is chosen, which is great. If this does not happen, the art director has to fit the sets into the available space, which is frequently too small.

A Sound Idea

The stage must be soundproof if sound recording is to be done. The stage walls and ceiling are padded with thick layers of sound-absorbing material. When filming or taping is in progress, a warning bell rings and lights flash outside the stage.

Did You Pay the Light Bill?

The lighting designer must have an adequate supply of electricity and places to hang the lighting instruments. One way to ensure this is to use the traditional motion picture system, which is to suspend platforms above the sets and fasten the lighting instruments to the hanging platforms. Lights on floor stands clutter the stage floor. Another way, more commonly used for video production, in which the cameras need to move about the stage floor, is to hang the lights from a permanently installed grid of pipes suspended from the stage ceiling. The lighting technicians use ladders to take the lights to the grid, where they are fastened. The most convenient system is to use pipes that are suspended by cables from pulleys fastened to the stage ceiling. The lines pass over the pulley wheels to the stage walls, where they are attached to a counterweight system that allows the pipes to be lowered to a few feet off the floor, where the lights can be attached to the pipes. The pipes carrying the lights are then raised to their working height above the set.

The Stage Floor

Some stages have rough wood floors. If this is the case, the art director has to cover the floor by building a false floor above it or by covering it with sheets of composition board or plywood. Some stages used primarily for video work have highly polished vinyl floors that blend smoothly into the cyclorama, a vertical surface made of plaster, wood, or cloth. The cyclorama, or *cyc* for short, is usually painted to match the floor, creating a horizonless effect. The cyclorama and floor can be bathed with colored light to change their colors, or they can be painted.

THE ALL-SEEING EYE (ALMOST)

The camera's job is to convert light energy into electrical energy. An important fact for the art director to consider is that the camera doesn't see as our eyes do. Our eyes can take in a very wide angle of vision, but the camera sees a much more limited field. The *aspect ratio* is the proportion of the picture, the relationship of height to width. The television picture ratio is 1.33:1, that is, one and thirty-three hundredths units wide and one unit high. Designers need to keep in mind that the outer edges of the picture are sometimes lost in transmission, so graphics and lettering should be kept away from the edges of the picture. Theatrical motion picture film formats take in a wider, more horizontal field of vision than video cameras do. Wide-screen formats commonly use a 2.35:1 ratio.

Remember Close-ups and Wide Shots

To get a sense of how the world looks to the video camera eye, cut a three-by-four-inch horizontal hole in a piece of cardboard. Hold it in front of one eye and observe your surroundings. Notice how your attention is drawn to a small area at a time and how the pictures you see become a series of compositions. You are not aware of the whole room or landscape. No matter how lavish the set when seen as a whole, don't forget the small areas in your million-dollar set or you may get a $1.98 close-up.

What does this aspect of the camera mean to the art director? It means that we have to make a room interior, for example, more compact than we would if we were interior designers for a room to be lived in. Cameras make a scene look more spacious than it appears to the eye. If you design a room the same size as you would for a living space, on camera it may look like the civic auditorium with some furniture stuck in it.

The Eye with Blinders

The video 3 to 4 ratio rectangle can't take in the whole world at once, but because the camera forces us to look at a confined area, we tend to examine that area with more focused interest. The crooked picture, the potted plant that seems to grow out of an actor's head, the high-backed chair that makes an actor seem to have sprouted wings all are common juxtapositions that may be unnoticed in a real room, but that draw attention to themselves on camera.

Now that you know where your work is going to be housed and what to expect technically, we will look at the basic elements of sets.

4

SCENIC BUILDING BLOCKS

As we saw earlier, pioneering movie producers relied heavily on theatrical tradition, adapting plays and staging techniques to the new film medium. Film and video set designers built upon traditional methods as well, adding more sophisticated materials and techniques as they became available.

TYPES OF FLATS AND MATERIALS

Softwall Flats

In the traditional theater, where lightweight, easily transportable scenery is an asset, the basic flat, or wall surface, is a wood framework covered with painted fabric. This method of scenic construction has evolved through centuries of experience and is ideal for theatrical purposes. Under the controlled conditions available on a theater stage, the light weight and reasonable cost of this form of construction are assets. Not all theatrical scenery is made this way, however. When rigidity and durability are required, scenery made of wood, metal, and synthetic materials is used, much the same as in motion picture and video work. The traditional *softwall* flat is used in motion picture and video work where rigidity and durability are not important. Ceiling pieces that are hung over the tops of sets can be made of muslin stretched over a wood frame. Light weight is an advantage in this case. Walls that are only seen through doorways and need not bear close scrutiny can be made this way, also, as well as small sky backings and scenic backdrops.

Hardwall Flats

Basic wood flats are made of a framework of 1" x 3" wood set on edge. Lumber sizes are named by the measurements of the rough wood before it is planed down to a smooth finish. The 1" x 3" dimensions become 3/4" x

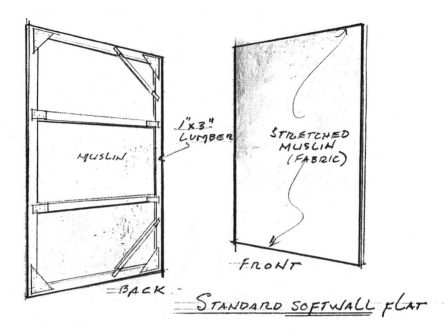

1"x3" LUMBER

MUSLIN

STRETCHED MUSLIN (FABRIC)

FRONT

BACK

STANDARD SOFTWALL FLAT

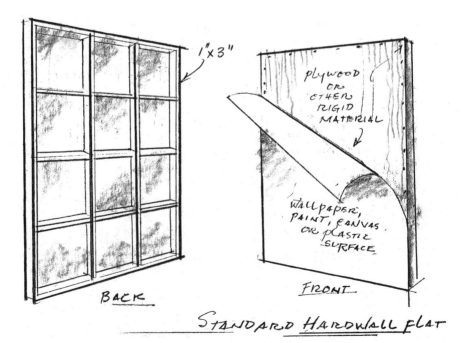

1"x3"

PLYWOOD OR OTHER RIGID MATERIAL

WALLPAPER, PAINT, CANVAS OR PLASTIC SURFACE

BACK

FRONT

STANDARD HARDWALL FLAT

2 3/4" after the wood is finished. The 1" x 3" lumber is set on edge and made into a grid, each square of which measures 24" x 24" on the centers of the lumber. A skin, or covering of plywood or composition board, is nailed and glued to one side of the framework, which is built to the desired height and width. Standard width for these flats is from twelve inches to eight feet, in one-foot progressions, and standard heights range from six feet to fourteen feet.

When this *hardwall* method of construction is used, the flats can be used repeatedly for longer than the frames covered with muslin. The plywood skin can be taken off and replaced, or other materials, such as vacuum-formed plastic sheets, can be stapled, nailed, or glued to the framework. The surface can be painted and papered many times. Hardwall flats also provide a sturdy surface for fastening light fixtures and picture hooks.

PLATFORMS

Platforms are used primarily to provide changes in floor level and can be made with metal framing as well as wood. Traditional theatrical platforms use folding bases called parallels, which are made of 1" x 12" or 1" x 3" wood frames with hinges at the corners that allow the units to fold and store easily. The tops of this type of platform are made of sheets of plywood that fit the parallels when they are unfolded. Standard sizes begin at 4' x 4' and go up to 4' x _10'. Parallel base heights commonly begin at six inches and go up in progressions to four feet.

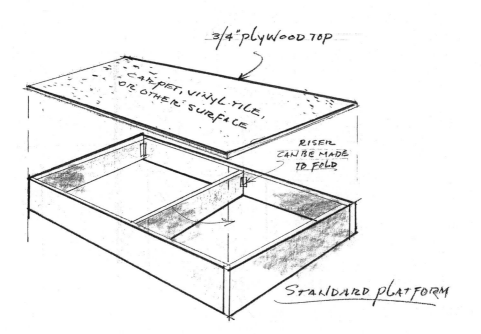

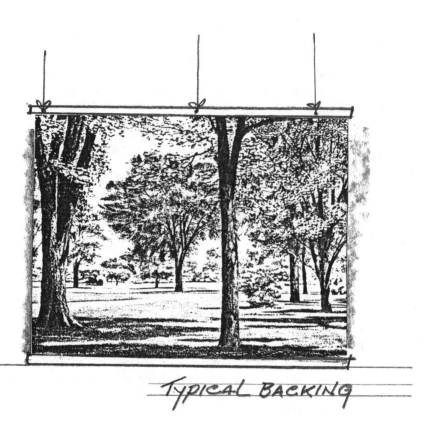

Typical Backing

Combinations of these sizes are put together to form raised areas. If an area is required that cannot be made of stock platforms, new construction is done to order, which is more expensive than working with stock sizes. Metal framing is used when unusual durability and strength are required. Platforms can be carpeted, surfaced with vinyl tile, or covered with composition board. If hard-surfaced platforms produce a rumbling sound when walked upon, sound-deadening material is applied to the inside of the unit.

BACKINGS

Backgrounds, which are sometimes called backdrops, are another type of basic scenery. Backings are used to present a large area of scenic background such as a landscape or city vista. They can be as high as the stage will accommodate. Large backings are painted on widths of muslin that have strips of wood called *battens* at the top and bottom. The painted muslin can be rolled on the battens for storage and transport.

Day and Night Backings

Day-and-night backings have translucent windows and skies that are painted with dyes rather than opaque paint. When a night effect is desired, diffuse lighting is directed through the translucent areas from the back, producing the appearance of lighted windows and a light or starry sky. When lit from the front, the effect is that of daylight.

Film Backings

Another type of backing is produced photographically on large sheets of translucent film. The image is like a giant color slide. These backings must be lit with diffuse light from the back, whether they depict day or night, and require more space than backings lit only from the front.

MATERIALLY SPEAKING

Wood is the major material used for scenery construction. Regular finished lumber is used in the same way it is used in other forms of construction. Plywood finds extensive use for large areas, particularly in the construction of flats and platforms. Fir plywood is used for the tops of platforms and for the skin of flats. Luan mahogany plywood, which has a smooth surface, is used where light weight and flexibility around curves are important.

Wood Grain

When a wood-grain appearance is called for, it is sometimes better to have a skilled scenic artist paint the appropriate texture and pattern on a surface than to use real wood. Some wood grains do not photograph well, particularly the dark colors and small patterns. A good scenic artist can emphasize the character and color of wood grains so that they read better on camera than the real thing.

Surface Materials

Many other materials are used for surfacing flats. Papier-mâché patterns, vacuum-formed plastic sheets, Mylar film, and textured fabrics are available in a great variety of color, pattern, and texture. Fire regulations require that all materials be used in a manner that allows flame support. If in doubt about any material with which you are unfamiliar, check the fire regulations covering the stage where the set will be standing.

SPECIAL EFFECTS SCENERY

Blue Screen

Some scenic elements are not built full size out of wood, metal, or synthetic materials. The background may be a painting, motion picture, or a scale

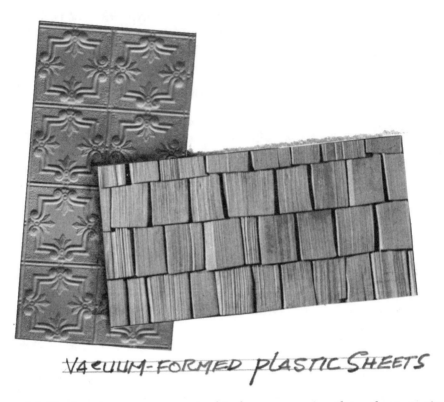

V4CUUM-FORMED plASTIC SHEETS

model. If actors in a car are required to be seen passing through an exotic locale, for example, stock film footage or new film shot of the location can be inserted behind the actors and car by the blue-screen method. The actors seated in the car are placed in front of a large area of saturated blue color background. The action is photographed as the car is rocked to simulate movement of a vehicle passing over the road surface. Blue area shows through the windows of the car and around it. The film processing laboratory, with the use of a filter, makes a piece of film that turns the blue areas into a black mask. An optical printer takes in the black-mask film and the background film and makes a composite print of the actors and the background.

The blue-screen process is similar in principle to the Chromakey effect used in video photography, as described later in the chapter on news-broadcast staging.

Models and Miniatures

Live action can also appear to take place in a scale model of a setting by photographing the model and action separately and combining the two images in an optical printer.

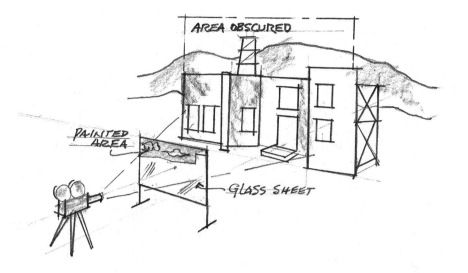

Matte Painting

Another type of nonbuilt scenery is matte painting. If, for example, a wide-angle shot of a street on a studio back lot is required, with action in the foreground, but oil derricks or a housing development show on the hillside beyond, an artist can paint the continuation of the buildings and a sky on a sheet of glass placed in front of the camera. This technique requires that the camera is placed in exactly the right position and that the artist can block in the painted area on the glass. The painting and scene can also be photographed separately, as in blue screen, and the images combined by the laboratory optical printer.

Now that we know the main physical foundations of settings, the next step is to cast light upon them. One of the most creative tools with which an art director works is *lighting*. Without the help of lighting instruments, lighting directors, and directors of photography, our hours and weeks of creative effort will be in vain. In the next chapter we will see how lighting works.

5

LIGHTING

After a set has been built and is standing on the stage, it needs to be carefully lit to make it visible to the cameras and to give it mood and atmosphere. The art director with a basic knowledge of lighting instruments and techniques can work with the lighting director or director of photography to bring out the set's quality. We will see what instruments produce different qualities of light and how they are controlled.

TWO TYPES OF LIGHTING INSTRUMENTS

Light produced by lighting instruments has two basic qualities: diffuse and focused. Diffuse light covers a broad area and is flat, such as the light given off by a bare frosted lightbulb or sunlight on a cloudy day. Focused light is directional, such as the beam of a flashlight.

Diffuse Lighting Instruments

Scoop—A large bulb in a scoop-shaped reflector
Broad—A group of lamps set next to each other on a flat white surface
Softlight—The lamp is hidden from view, reflecting off a white surface
Striplight—A row of lamps used to illuminate large areas of backings or
   walls with diffused light

Directional Lighting Instruments

This group of lights gives the lighting director control over the direction and shape of the light beam.

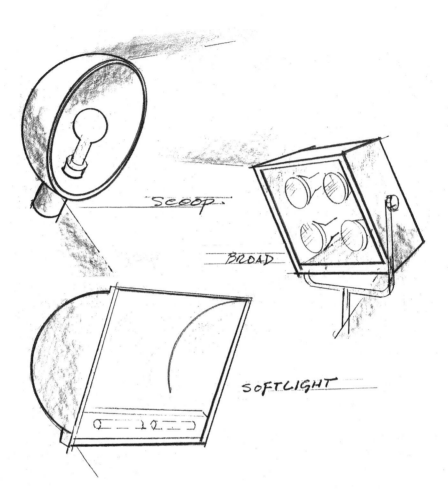

Scoop

BROAD

SOFTLIGHT

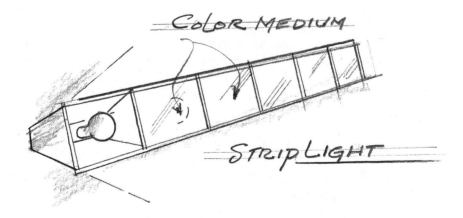

Color MEDIUM

StripLIGHT

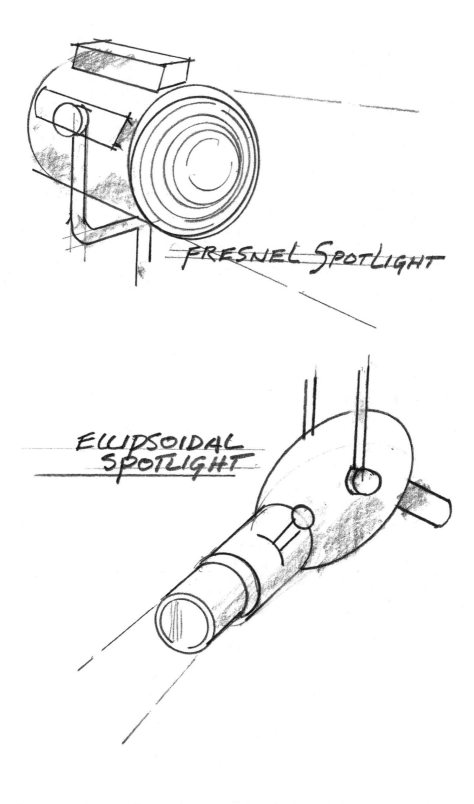

FRESNEL SPOTLIGHT

ELLIPSOIDAL SPOTLIGHT

Fresnel (freh-nel) spotlight—After struggling with the old thick glass spotlight lenses, which were inefficient and tended to shatter and fall on actors' heads, Agustin-Jean Fresnel invented the Fresnel lens that, through a series of concentric ridges, overcame these difficulties and immortalized the name Fresnel. This light produces a beam that can be shaped.

Ellipsoidal spotlight—This light can produce a sharply defined beam of light. It gets its name from the elliptically shaped reflector inside the housing. Metal slides can be placed inside the lens housing to cast patterns and shapes on the set surfaces.

LIGHT CONTROLS

Up in the grid are long strips of electrical outlets, called power rails. Each lighting instrument hanging from the grid or counterweighted pipe is plugged into a numbered outlet in the power rail. The circuits are connected to a patch panel where groups of lighting instruments can be connected to sets of dimmers that control the amount of electricity flowing through the lamp filaments, producing the desired degree of brightness.

Barndoors

Each of the Fresnel-lensed spotlights has a set of four black metal flaps, called *barndoors,* attached in front of the lens. These flaps can be adjusted to shape the light beam.

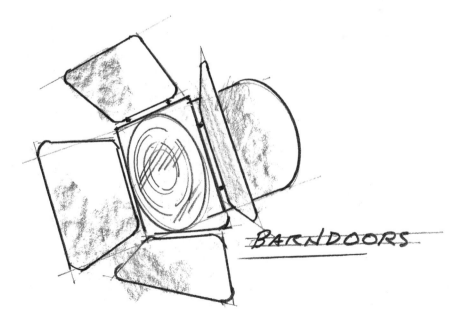

BARNDOORS

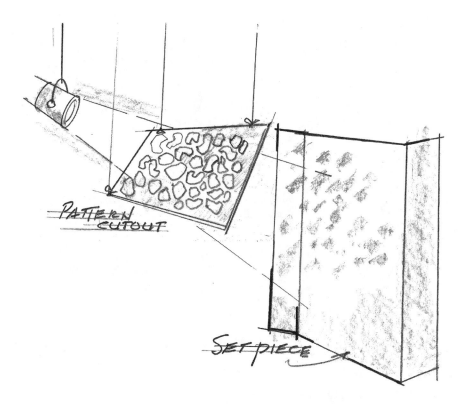

PATTERN CUTOUT

SET PIECE

Color

Another means of light control is the use of color. A metal frame holds a sheet of plastic film, available in hundreds of colors.

Patterns

To produce soft patterns on surfaces, the lighting technicians place a cutout called a *cookie* (after a man named Cukaloris) a few feet in front of a spotlight. These plywood or metal cutouts can carry patterns of venetian blinds, foliage, or abstract designs, breaking up an otherwise flat-lit wall.

Flags

To control the spread of a light beam farther outside the lens, a piece of opaque black fabric stretched over a rectangular rod frame can be placed on a stand in front of the lighting instrument. The flag can be adjusted easily to block off light from an area.

REFLECTOR

Silks and Reflectors

The unclouded sun produces harsh light. This light is not particularly flat-tering to actors and creates dark shadows, which many directors of photog-raphy and lighting directors do not like. Every location company carries silver-foil or white-surfaced 5′ x 5′ panels that are placed on stands to reflect sunlight into the unwanted shadows.

For larger areas of diffused sunlight, 20′ x 20′ or larger panels of translu-cent white fabric, called *silks*, or lengths of mesh are stretched over the area to soften the light.

Now that we have seen the basic tools with which a lighting director works, two lighting directors will demonstrate their methods of set lighting. See which one you want to light your set.

6

TECHNIQUES FOR EFFECTIVE LIGHTING

Film lighting techniques differ from video lighting methods. In film, the director of photography (DP), after discussing the mood, style, and general look of the photography with the director, shoots tests using various lenses, filters, and film stocks. When these elements are determined, the DP directs the hanging of lights, and, with an exposure meter, balances the lighting quality and intensities. As film photography usually uses only one camera and many changes of angle, the DP directs the relighting and touching up of the lighting on the actors and set between camera setups.

The video lighting director confers with the director and video technicians to provide the correct light levels for the dramatic effect and the electronic system. When three or four video cameras are used, the director cuts from camera to camera without stopping to relight each time. The lighting director, then, has to light the actors and set to accommodate the different angles as the director cuts from camera to camera.

LIGHTING THE ACTORS

Lighting directors commonly use the triangular lighting system for the actors: *key light, backlight,* and *fill light,* unless dramatic mood lighting is called for.

Key light—A spotlight, usually a Fresnel-lensed instrument, is used for the main light from the front or from a slight angle. This light defines the forms, showing the hollows, high points, and textures.

Backlight—Another spotlight is hung above and behind the actor. It separates the actor from the background with light of a higher intensity than on the background.

Fill light—This is usually provided by a *broad, scoop,* or *softlight.* Its purpose is to fill in the shadows cast by the key light so that the camera will see some detail in the shadows.

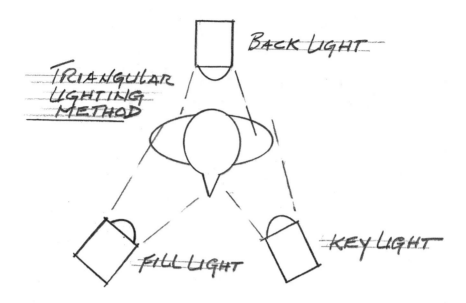

DIFFERENT LIGHTING METHODS

Lighting directors Jones and Smith will now demonstrate two ways of using diffuse and directional lighting instruments. Besides having to light the set, they also have to light the actors. Both lighting people have consulted the director, who has told them where the actors will be and where they will move, as well as the time of day, which is dusk in this example. Each lighting director, light meter in hand, will stand in the set at the appropriate places, directing the lighting technicians who hang and focus the lights for the actors and the set.

The Jones Method

Jones floods the walls of our lovingly designed smart suburban living room set with the required amount of light per square foot, roams the set with his light meter, calls the set lit, and goes to lunch. This approach gets Jones and his crew to lunch early and makes the meters in the camera control system register the correct numbers, but causes much complaining from the director and art director. Jones, however, believes that he has done his job.

The Jones Result

When we look at the set lit by the Jones method, the roof of the house in which the room is supposed to be seems to have been ripped off, and brilliant shadowless light floods the interior. The script says the time of day is dusk, and the heroine is expecting the neighbors to drop over and admire her new sofa. Bright light at this time of day makes no sense at all. Besides, after we have carefully designed nooks and crannies into this room and have rummaged around through junkyards to find terrific old moldings to go around the doors, the carving is hardly visible on the monitor picture, and the set walls are as flat as cardboard. The Jones method has destroyed the character and mood of the set.

The Smith Method

Enter lighting director Smith. She lights the actors in the same manner as Jones did, using key lights, backlights, and fill lights, but the key lights are not quite as strong as Jones's key lights, and the backlight comes from the direction of the picture window. Great. Things are looking up. At least we can see where the light is coming from.

Smith directs some low-angle light through the front window and at the outside of the front door so that when the neighbors come over and step through the door, they are backlit with what we quickly perceive to be the rays of the lowering sun, giving us a clue as to the time of day. Smith also places a metal slide in an ellipsoidal spotlight that casts the shadow of a window frame on the opposite wall. Here is another clue for the audience that it's late in the day, when the sun is low in the sky. To prepare for scenes that are to take place in full daylight, Smith sets the light levels on the backing outside the window somewhat higher than those inside the set. The computer-controlled lighting system stores the data for the two different lighting effects.

Enter: Motivated Lighting
We have placed some lamps at decorative places in the room. Jones treated them as he did every other object in the set: more things to reflect light to make the meters point to the right numbers. Smith replaces the fifty-watt bulbs with which the lamps came from the prop house with 150-watt bulbs that give more light. She then connects the lamps to a dimmer circuit so that, if the director decides to have our sofa-hostess draw the drapery in front of the picture window when the sun has set, the lighting director can bring up the intensity of the lamps to put across the idea that night has fallen. Already the room looks as if someone lives in it.

Firmly Ensconsed
Included in the set dressing is a pair of wall sconces that flank a painting. Some lighting directors, the minute their eyes land on the wall sconces, will direct a small spotlight on the sconce. Not only does this light cast a glow on the wall, which is just fine, but the bulbs in the sconces cast their own shadows on the wall, which in reality is quite impossible for even the finest wall sconce to do.

Having fallen into this trap once, early in her career, Smith avoids it by hanging a small spotlight up in the grid, just as Jones did. Smith, however, has the light coming down at a sharp angle so that it misses the sconce and casts only a homey glow on the wall. What she has is a wall sconce not casting its own shadow.

Smith turns her attention to the other walls. She has sensitivity and taste, noticing that we have spent a lot of time finding the right moldings to go around the doors. She isn't going to let them go to waste as Jones did. Using just enough light from motivated sources such as the table lamps, wall sconces, and setting sun, Smith brings out the three-dimensional quality of the room's shapes by casting shadows, without letting the lighting call attention to itself. We don't want the lighting or the set to distract the audience from the ravings of the actors while the scene is in progress.

Three Cheers for Smith!

When Smith finishes lighting, the set looks three-dimensional, the audience will know the time of day, the actors will look good, and our junkyard moldings will tell the audience something about the house resident's taste. What more could anyone ask? Answer: a raise for lighting director Smith.

LOCATION LIGHTING

The examples have shown how lighting directors can make or break a set on a stage. They can do the same on location, where space is usually more limited.

Let us say that our living room is in a real house that is rented for the shoot period. The time of day and action are the same and the medium is video. As video does not have to use filters for combinations of daylight and artificial light, the lighting director does not have to compensate for both with color-correction mediums in front of the lights. Both film and video, though, have to light the room from floor-mounted stands, as the room has a ceiling and no grid from which to hang lights. Also, the light sources have to be cleverly hidden in less space than is available on a stage, so much ingenuity is called for to produce a natural effect. Generators provide electricity, requiring long runs of electrical cable.

Film directors of photography select film stock, lens filters, and corrective filtering media that are taped to the outside of windows to correct the color temperature, balancing with the added interior lighting. In some cases, the lights are filtered instead, for use as daylight.

The art director's concern with the mood of lighting on location is the same as for stage work, but tempered with the inherent difficulties of location. Location shooting frequently has to match stage work, so the art director has to be on the alert. A lighting director may take the easy way out, as Jones did with his flat lighting, pleading lack of space, but the art director can help Jones change his approach.

The art director or production designer, then, not only designs the sets and supervises their construction and setup but is concerned with how the lighting director or director of photography brings out the sets' best qualities.

Now that we have some familiarity with lighting, let's meet two important people with whom the art director works: the producer and the director.

Part II

OUTLINE OF
A JOB

Now that we understand the role of the production designer, Part II traces the progress of a design project from getting the job to evaluating the results.

We will meet the producer and director, read the script, analyze the set needs, and learn how to do visual research. Then, based on what we know about the characters and their environments, we will make a sketch of the set and create construction drawings and a model, following easy-to-understand illustrations. We will follow the set through construction, setup on the stage, and set decoration, and will see where we succeeded and where we can improve.

MEET THE PRODUCER
AND DIRECTOR

At last! A job! After many days of not making any noise at all, the phone rings. A producer wants to talk to you about a project. Those business cards you had printed and passed out to everybody on the set during your last job have paid off.

The producer and director generate the production and style of a film and are the two most important people with whom the production designer and art director work. They control the way the production begins and progresses. We will see how to collaborate with the producer and director and some questions to ask of them.

THE PRODUCER

First, the producer has to have an idea or script to produce. This can be his own property or may be purchased from someone else. Second, the producer has to have money with which to produce the epic. Some daring producers who have no money will try to raise the money with the help of your talent and work. Beware if you hear either of the following plans.

Plan A: The Points Plan

After describing how exciting this project is going to be, the producer will ask you to do some sketches. In exchange for your work, you will share in the vast profits of the venture; that is, you will get points (a percentage) of the money that will come rolling in. It is best to say that you are late for another appointment and to leave immediately when you hear talk like this, unless you are desperate for something to do that is not rewarding, have a rich uncle who pays your rent, or are compulsively anxious about building up your portfolio samples. If the latter, be sure to make copies of your work, because you will never see the originals again.

Plan B: The Check Is in the Mail

The would-be producer will claim that the production money is in the bank, and that all you have to do is design the sets, send a bill, and a check will be in the mail the same day. Since you do not know how familiar this person is with the bank or the mailbox, prudently ask for a portion of your fee in advance, and the remainder upon completion of your work. If this producer shifts uneasily in the executive chair and says that you can trust him, don't. Again, leave gracefully unless you want to look for the imaginary check in the mailbox for the next two years.

Now that you have heard about a couple of types to avoid, here's the way a legitimate producer works. When the producer has decided that you are the right person for the job, discuss a fee for your services. Sensitive souls that we are, most of us dread this part, but based on your track record, talent, and experience, and keeping in mind the twenty-four-hour-a-day nature of show work, state the amount you feel the job is worth. Ask the producer how much is budgeted for your work.

The Set Budget

An experienced producer has arrived at a budget figure for set construction, based on the needs of the production. As you have not read the script and do not know what the set requirements are, make a note of the figure as a guide while you are designing the sets and assembling costs.

An inexperienced producer may not have worked out a set budget, expecting you to provide the numbers. Be prepared to provide this information early on during your work so there are no misunderstandings later. As the production gets under way, the producer may start cutting corners and moving money from one department to another. One of the first cuts is frequently the art department.

Negotiate in a realistic way, but don't agree to work below your level. When you and the producer agree, ask for a letter of agreement or a contract spelling out the conditions and payment schedule. This piece of paper will be helpful if your payment doesn't show up and the producer seems reluctant to answer your phone calls.

Above- and Below-the-Line Personnel

What is this line that some people are above and some below? Two separate budgets are prepared for most productions: one for the creative people who generate the ideas on which the show is based, and one for the technical personnel and facilities. Each person or department, including the art department, creates and submits a detailed budget, listing individual items. If an independent producer is going to make a deal in which the producer will provide the creative staff and the studio will provide the technical people and facilities, it is convenient to separate the two groups.

Some of the above-the-line categories are producer, associate producer, writer, director, actors, art director, and composer.

Some of the below-the-line categories are video engineers, camera operators, lighting technicians, stage manager, audio engineer, stage facilities, construction, and props.

The producer's job is to oversee all phases of production, and to make sure that everything is going according to plan. The job is to *produce*. When things aren't going right (they rarely do) the producer must be able to regroup the forces.

THE DIRECTOR

Each director works with the production designer or art director in a different way. If the project is very elaborate, with many sets and locations, the director may want very detailed storyboards depicting each camera setup. Some directors prefer to spend the bulk of their time working with the actors' performances and are not so concerned with their environments, so they may not want a lot of assistance.

Film Direction

The film director usually works with one camera and an assistant director or two, who handle the operation of the company working on the stage or location. The film director studies the script, breaks it down into elements, creates the shooting schedule, and works with the film editor as well as the director of photography.

Video Direction

The video director's job is more technically oriented. Let's take the example of a production that has several sets on a stage, four video cameras, and actors involved in a drama. Before entering the dimly lit control room, the video director does some homework, just as the film director does.

1.   Studies the script
2.   Determines the approach
3.   Prepares a shooting schedule

4. Does camera blocking
5. Rehearses actors off and on the set

Seated beside or near the director are an assistant director, the associate producer perhaps, the technical crew chief (who can also be the video switcher), a sound mixer, and a production assistant or two. Facing these people are banks of video monitors, each showing images from cameras, film projectors, computer graphics storage, slides, and videotape: a menu from which the director chooses. Everyone in the control booth can talk and hear each other through headsets. The stage manager is the director's representative on the stage.

Assuming that you and the director have not taken an instant dislike to each other, it is wise to find out what the director has in mind. This effort in the beginning can save lots of headaches and shrieks of rage later.

Questions to Ask

Here are some questions to ask the director:

How do you see the style of the show?
Do you want composition and camera angle suggestions?
What mood do you want to emphasize?
Have you any color loves or hates?

The sooner you confer with the director, the better. In the case of some film projects prepared for television, the director's time is contracted for a minimum number of preparation and shooting days, so the art director may not have much opportunity for preproduction conference time.

Style

Most directors will know how they want to shoot the show. If the story contains a lot of action, the pace will be fast. The art director probably won't have to put a lot of character-defining objects in the sets. A Gothic drama would seem to call for somber colors and lots of gloom, but the director may want to reject this obvious approach.

She may say, "I see the darkness in the characters and not in their surroundings. I want to surround them with lightness to emphasize that mood." See what would have happened had you not found that out? You might have spent days working up the gloomiest ruined castles to be found anywhere, only to discover that the director wanted something else.

Color

Color is a subjective area, and it is risky to assume that everyone is going to like the colors you think are right. It is rarely possible to reason with anyone in matters of taste, but try anyway. If you can drag out some good reasons for choosing the colors you did, by all means parade them by and try to convince the doubters, in a diplomatic manner, that your choices are appropriate ones. Be willing to listen to the director's opinions as well.

Budget

When discussing the production with the producer and director, ask specific questions about the budget. Some companies require the art director to sign off, that is, sign an agreement that states the amount of money the art director and staff cannot exceed without further approval. With experience comes a sense of costs. The wise art director gets specific costs from suppliers before committing dollar amounts and keeps careful daily accounts as the money goes out.

So now we have met two more variables, the producer and director, who have signed up to do a half-hour video pilot, which is described in the next chapter.

HERE'S THE VIDEO SCRIPT

We are going to work for a not very affluent producer who will try to cut corners. The script does not arrive richly bound in plastic leather with gold embossed lettering. It has paper covers and is bound with three brass fasteners, the removal of which will allow placement in a loose-leaf binder. The title and author's name are printed on the first page, as well as the series title, episode title and number, the producer's name, and the copyright notice.

ANALYZING THE SCRIPT

Freely read the script without making notes. Images of the characters and their environments will form in your mind. These pictures are the visual foundation of a unified production design.

Settings

Leafing through the dialogue, we pause at blocks of text that describe the sets and locations.

```
INTERIOR—PATTY'S LIVING ROOM
INTERIOR—RICHARD'S OFFICE
INTERIOR—MRS. HARRISON'S KITCHEN
EXTERIOR—THE TOWN PARK
INTERIOR—A HOTEL ROOM IN SWEDEN
```

Small Towns and Flashbacks
We also learn that the story locale is a small town in central Iowa named Erling, population 500. The time is the present, except for the scene in Mrs.

Harrison's kitchen, which is a flashback to 1938, and the scene in the Swedish hotel room, which took place five years ago. To begin sorting out the elements relevant to our part of the production, take a look at the two main characters.

Characters

Meet Patty Johanssen

The writer has provided us with a character sketch of Patty. "Patty Johanssen, twenty-six, is the mayor of a small town in Iowa. Patty is a self-reliant young woman, an orphan since she was fourteen, when her parents were atomized in a grain elevator explosion. Patty lives in the old family home just off Main Street. She became the mayor a few months ago when she decided that someone should revive her withering hometown. She ran for the office and won the election, much to the chagrin of the town elders, who are a source of conflict."

Now that we have some facts about the central character, ask some questions about her environment.

1. What does a small town in Iowa look like?
2. What does an old family home in a small town in Iowa look like?
3. What would have happened to that house in the seventy-five years since it was built that would give the audience for our epic the message that the house is that old?
4. What kind of modernization would be visible?
5. What objects would Patty have collected inside the house that would tell the audience about her occupation, taste, and general character?

Here Is Richard

Richard has left the big city of Chicago to pursue the good life of a small-town newspaper publisher. He is unrealistic about the prejudices and traditions of small-town life, a source of conflict between him and Patty. Richard is twenty-nine years old, and he and Patty talk of getting married someday. Richard lives in the back room of the small building that houses his office and printing plant.

Now that we know a little about Richard, let's visualize his surroundings.

1. What does a small-town publisher's office look like?
2. Would Richard's office be typical, based on what we know about his character?
3. What objects would be in his living quarters?

DOING RESEARCH

Other than being given transportation and an expense account to go to Iowa, which our tight-fisted producer is not going to provide, we have to look for visual information somewhere.

Some art directors keep their own research collections. This is fine if you are willing to spend the time and money to maintain such a collection, but most people aren't. Also, it is impossible for any individual to collect enough material to cover all needs. Most art directors have some visual material collected from previous projects that may come in handy again. Most art directors keep basic books such as architectural standards, lettering, atlases, pictorial encyclopedias, and volumes of interest to the individual.

How About Your Library Card?

Most sizable public libraries maintain picture files in the reference sections. These files contain photographs and illustrations from magazines. Remember that an illustrator's view of a small town in Iowa can be misleading, compared to a documentary photograph. A painting can give valuable hints on color and composition but does not necessarily represent the reality that should be the starting point for designing our own version. Original sources are best.

Also, the cataloging systems used in libraries may hide the pictures we are looking for because they are set up primarily for *word* use rather than *picture* use.

Specialized Libraries

In the early days of motion picture production this problem cropped up, so the studios assembled their own libraries of specialized visual material. These libraries not only contained word material for the use of writers but held pictures for the use of art directors and set designers. A few of the remaining major studios have retained their libraries. Others have sold their research facilities to individuals who continue to provide research service.

Look Out for the Toaster Experts

When looking for research material and using it, be assured that someone in the viewing audience will notice an error in time placement. Someone will notice the 1955 toaster in a 1949 kitchen. Use objects and decorating styles that were present *before* or contemporary with the period in which you are working, but never *after* the period, because these objects and styles would not have existed then.

Sears, Wards, and Spiegel

As indicators of objects and styles in current use during a specific period, the popular mail-order catalogs are very useful. They accurately reflect mass taste and provide guides to common objects such as stoves, beds, furniture, and bric-a-brac. Family photo albums are rich sources of reality.

Don't Take Anyone's Word for It

When doing research, there is no substitute for *original sources, firsthand observation,* and *the camera.* Don't guess what something looks like. Some extra time spent finding out what reality is will pay off. Then put your own interpretation on the visual material.

The information gathered so far is general information for further scrutiny, as you will see in the next chapter.

USING YOUR RESEARCH

Now that you have a pile of research material staring you in the face, the time has come to sort it. There it is: books, photographs, clippings, fabric samples, color chips, a family album, and some catalogs. The first thing to do is organize it so that you can find what you will need during the process of designing each set. Here are some general categories:

Iowa, general landscape
Small towns (general)
Houses, exterior (Patty)
Houses, interior (Patty)
Newspaper offices (Richard)
Kitchens, 1938 (Mrs. Harrison)
Parks, small town
Hotel rooms, Sweden

Go through the pile and place the material in the subject-labeled folders. While making sketches, you will then be able to find individual categories without having to sift through the entire stack each time you are looking for something. Clear some flat space in your vast studio or kitchen dinette where you can lay out the folders, boxes, and books in orderly fashion, so that instant help will be available when inspiration strikes.

IOWA, GENERAL LANDSCAPE

For this project, the general landscape material will be of limited use because most of the sets are interiors. If this were a film feature, this file would be one of the largest because a film production on location would be concerned with the appearance of the landscape more than a studio production with interior sets. The most we will need to see of the landscape will be some glimpses through windows and doors, and in the park scenes, which will be done on the stage. If individual houses in exterior photography are identified as places where specific characters live, you will need to get detailed photographs of these places from many angles in case you have to reproduce portions of the structures on the stage. The general landscape folder will be useful when it's time to find some backings to use outside the doors and windows.

SMALL TOWNS (GENERAL)

The material in this folder is similar in nature to the general landscape material, but it shows buildings and architectural style and detail. Keep these pictures waiting in the wings for use as background.

HOUSES, EXTERIOR (PATTY)

Look for the forms of the houses, the materials with which they are surfaced, and the colors and textures created by people and weather. Has the house been covered with aluminum siding, which is wider than the older wooden siding? Has the house been painted many times, and has the paint peeled off in places to reveal the former color? Is the architectural style of the house in keeping with Patty's background as you know it? What kinds of gutters,

downspouts, roof surfaces, and chimneys do you see? What kinds of shrub-bery grow around the house and yard? Is it well kept? Is there a sidewalk, and if so, is it in good condition or has a tree root pushed it up?

HOUSES, INTERIOR (PATTY)

Our study of the script tells us that only the front hall, the inside of the front door, and the living room will be needed for the pilot episode, so this infor-mation is your guide in looking through this folder. This does not mean that you cannot take elements from other rooms if they seem appropriate and useful for the two areas you need to create. Patty's living room would be a combination of old and new, as this is the house in which she has lived all her life. The room would probably contain old and new furniture and objects.

Look at the walls and windows. Houses change and have their own per-sonalities. Do you see a combination of tall older windows and large new aluminum-framed picture windows? Are the walls papered? What are the colors and patterns? Has someone installed printed wood panels over the old wall surfaces? What kinds of moldings are used for the baseboards, ceil-ing coving, and picture moldings? Are the floors carpeted wall to wall, or does the original old wood flooring show around the edges of a worn old floral-patterned carpet?

Study the ceilings, as you probably need to include a portion to keep the cameras from overshooting the back of the set. Observe the styles of furniture in the photographs. Perhaps the old sofa has been reupholstered in a contemporary fabric.

NEWSPAPER OFFICES (RICHARD)

Do you think that Richard, when he bought the newspaper, would have had the office painted, or would he have left the walls and equipment as he found them? His character description says that he is a combination of liberal and conservative and has traditional and contemporary tastes. To indicate this, you could place a computer typesetter beside the old Linotype machine, for example.

MRS. HARRISON'S KITCHEN (1938)

Research material shines when you are faced with designing a room from the past. It is possible to come fairly close to reality when working in the contemporary period with familiar scenes, but when dealing with the past, find reliable research material and scrutinize it carefully for the smallest objects. As we said before, watch out for objects that were made after the period in which you are working.

Most kitchens have windows. Pay attention to the ones in the photographs. You will need to have a backing outside the windows, so think about using a backyard fence in front of the painted neighborhood scene and perhaps a miniature water tower between the fence and the backing. If you calculate the size correctly, the little tower can appear to be a mile away from the fence. Refer to the script to see if the characters make entrances and exits through interior doors. If they do, provide suitable wild (movable) walls to be seen through the open doors.

PARKS, SMALL TOWN

These photographs provide a different sort of information. Instead of walls, floors, and ceilings, we have ground, sky, and vegetation. Exterior sets need much thought and skill to be convincing. If you try to get by with some plastic tree trunks and grass mats, the result will leave much to be desired and will spoil the believability of the scene. Select research material with examples of local vegetation, and come as close as possible to that. Remember that avocado trees do not grow in Iowa parks.

Don't try to create a forest. Create the illusion of park plants and trees with economical means such as foreground shrubbery and tree trunks that need not continue very far above the top camera frame line. If the planting does not have to be in place for more than a day or two, cared-for live plants in pots will survive. Realistic artificial plants are more practical. Chemically preserved natural foliage is available in larger production centers.

Look at the ground surfaces in the photographs. A park could have an area of gravel or a concrete picnic spot, which is a way to eliminate the wrinkled grass-mat approach. Some stages at large studios have real dirt floors, but as we will not have that advantage, think of ways to cover a vinyl-tile studio floor so that it looks like grass, dirt, or concrete.

What do you see beyond the ground surface? A possibility is a view of the town in the distance, depicted by a painted backing. Another would be the side of a park building.

If you decide to use a backing, think carefully about how to blend the ground surfaces into the painted scene so that the camera does not see an obvious line where the ground meets the sky. One way to do this is with an irregular row of shrubbery. Another way is to build up the ground surface into a gentle slope, placing bushes and plants that diminish in size from foreground to background. Be sure that when the lighting is done, none of the planting casts shadows on the sky. Think of some three-dimensional objects to place in the set to give the director and actors opportunities for action as well as making the environment more realistic. How about a set of swings, some teeter-totters, a slide, and some picnic tables? The director will be pleased if you do this.

HOTEL ROOMS, SWEDEN

Proceed the same way, from general to specific, with this set. The hotel would most likely be an old building. Find objects that say *Sweden* and feature them in the room. A tile corner stove and some contemporary furniture would be a start. What do Swedish windows look like? How are they different from American windows? If you can't find a backing depicting a Swedish city, perhaps you can have one painted from your research photographs. If this is not practical, put a hunk of tiled roof outside the window with the sky showing behind it. Would it be too much to put an appropriately sized Swedish flag showing above the roof? If the little water tower worked outside Mrs. Harrison's kitchen window, the flag might work for Sweden.

Now that we have some visual ideas rattling around in our heads, how do we put them together to make them visible to others? Turn to the next chapter and see.

MAKING SOME SKETCHES

The best way to put collected images together and communicate visual ideas to others is to make sketches. Don't labor over this part of the project too much. At first, just freely put your ideas on paper, successes and failures both, and the set sketch you want to show to your client will come together.

MATERIALS

Look over your supply of sketching materials. If you have none, or need more, the following will help you create a list to take to the art supply store

It's OK to Trace

Tracing paper is a must. If you work on opaque paper, you will end up transferring all the drawings to tracing paper anyway, because it is expensive and difficult to duplicate drawings in large sizes from opaque paper. Tracing paper allows you to draw away without the feeling that your work is carved in stone for the ages, and it is very easy to crumple up and hurl into the wastebasket when an idea doesn't seem as brilliant as you thought it was. The major sterling quality of tracing paper is that you can see through it. This quality makes it easy to resketch a previous drawing that has more good qualities than bad, and can be saved by tracing it to eliminate the bad stuff.

Don't Judge Paper by Its Cover
Tracing paper comes in rolls, sheets, and pads. While the price of a roll may seem high at first, it is the cheapest way in the end, because you are not paying for cutting, padding, and covers. You can tear off a piece of tracing paper just the right size by placing it under a metal edge or against the edge

of the kitchen table or you can cut it with scissors. It is not necessary to buy the finest-quality paper for making sketches or for preliminary construction drawings, no matter what the salesperson may say. Save the better-quality paper for final construction drawings because it will have to stand up to much erasing and travels through the printmaking machines.

A Little Talk About Pencils

Unless you feel insecure without a large jar bristling with pencils, all you really need for sketches is a soft 4B or 5B lead pencil. Soft lead works best because it provides little resistance to being zipped across the paper to give your slightest creative impulse free rein. Soft lead makes an easily reproducible line as well, and you can make great professional-looking smudges for shading. All you need for that is your thumb. Get an eraser of your choice. They come in dozens of colors and shapes, but be sure your favorite will really erase soft pencil lines.

Tape It Down

Put away the pushpins and tape the corners of an 18" x 24" piece of tracing paper to your drawing surface, which can be the back of a piece of mat

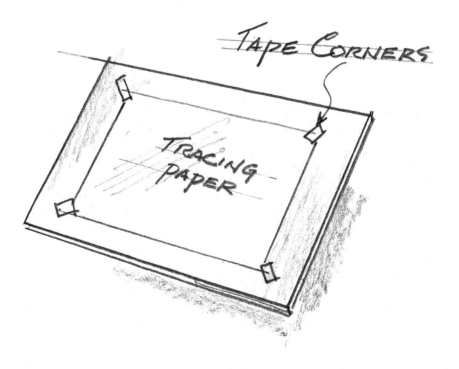

board taped to your drawing board or kitchen table. If you prefer, you need not tape the tracing paper down at the corners unless you want to use the T square and triangles. If your sketch is much smaller than 18" x 24", clients at production meetings will have difficulty seeing it from across the room. A reducing copy machine can make smaller versions of the sketch to place in notebooks if necessary.

PUTTING IDEAS ON PAPER

By this time you should have an idea of what you are going to do with the two required areas of Patty's house: the living room and hall. Because they are two parts of the same general set area, you have the opportunity to work in some interesting three-dimensional elements such as an arch or overhead beams that will give a sculptural look to the pictures. Remember that this is not a real house, and that the camera will see only the portions of the house you want it to see. The audience must sense that the rest of the house is there, but they just don't see it. One way to do this is to provide doors, which the audience assumes open into another room, unless this is a horror movie in which rich Aunt Myrtle has been bricked up behind the door to the dining room.

How Big?

Now you have to face the question of how big to make the set. Cameras make sets look larger than they appear to the eye, so if you want a wall to look ten feet wide, make it nine feet wide in your set. If you are unsure about the sizes of rooms, measure some familiar rooms at home for reference points. When making rough sketches of sets, don't worry too much about exact dimensions. Just have a general idea of size. When you have designed some sets and see them sitting grandly on the stage, you can compare the sketches and the finished work. The size-visualization process will become more natural each time you do this.

Remember that the producer and director are going to look at your sketches and receive an impression of size and mood. When they tell you to go ahead and make the construction drawings, you will need to come as close as you can to the impression received from your sketches. Otherwise, you will hear the dreaded words "I didn't know it was going to look like that!"

Draw Some Lines

The next step is to pencil in, lightly, the outlines of the room. If you do not do this and just start drawing at one corner of the paper, you will probably

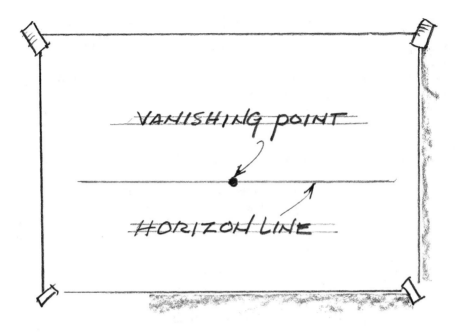

run out of room when you get to the other side or will finish the drawing with vast areas of unexplored territory. Regard this drawing as a preliminary sketch to clarify your thinking. If you want to sketch portions of the rooms and put them together in a composite sketch, that's OK too. The point is, when you wind up with a sketch that's ready to be viewed, your drawing should be roughly centered on the paper with some blank space around the edges.

One-Point Perspective

Slightly below the center of the paper, draw a horizon line from one side of the paper to the other. At the center of this line, make a dot. This dot represents the place our brains will perceive as the vanishing point: that is, where all the extended lines defining the tops and bottoms of the walls facing right and left will disappear over the horizon. In this simple perspective system, the lines representing the top and bottom of the back, or upstage, wall are parallel to the horizon line and are doomed to be parallel forever unless we move our viewpoint to one side or the other.

Draw a line about three inches above the horizon line to represent the top of the upstage wall, and draw another line about three inches below the horizon line to represent the bottom of the upstage wall. Then draw vertical lines showing where the wall ends on the right and the left. Leave room for the side walls, which will be in perspective. Think of the room as a box with no top and the front wall missing. You are looking into the open

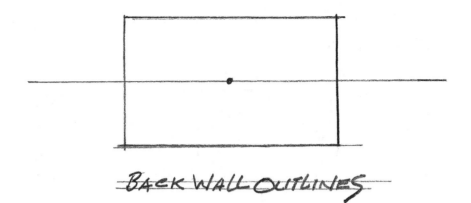

end. Draw a stylized figure of a person standing near the front of the room to help you visualize the size of the room.

Two More Walls

Two or three inches to the right and left of the ends of the back wall, draw vertical lines that extend above and below the top and bottom of the back wall. These lines are the ends of the walls closest to you as you look into the open-ended box of the room. Line up a triangle edge with the top of the line indicating the left wall edge and the dot on the horizon. Draw a line from the top of the wall to where the line meets the back wall. If you continue this line, which you may to help you understand the mystery of perspective, the line will theoretically disappear at the vanishing-point dot. Using the same system, draw the bottom of the left wall and the top and bottom of the right

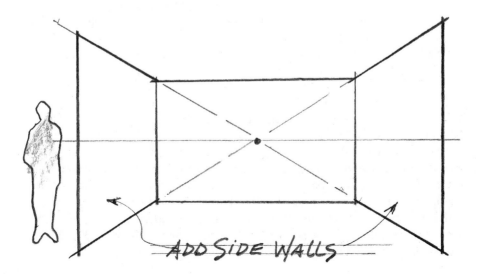

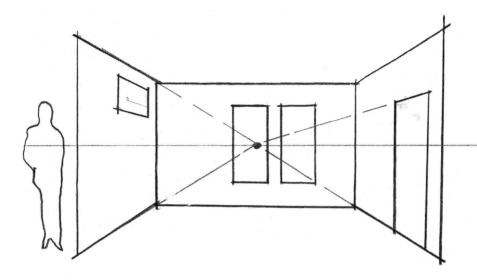

wall. Now you should have what looks like a three-sided box, if you have been paying attention and not gazing out the window.

What Do We Do with the Box?

Surely you can see that this is the beginning of a living room in a house in a small town in Iowa if you have any imagination at all. Now that you have established the main outlines of the room and are satisfied that it is about the right size compared with your little figure person, begin drawing in the doors and windows using the same system you used for the walls, remembering our friend the dot sitting there on the horizon line. Keep on using light lines because they are easier to erase when you want to change something. Don't draw a complete ceiling, but you might add a couple of beams and a back portion of the ceiling. A full ceiling for this type of production will not allow the lighting director convenient placement of the backlights referred to earlier.

Getting Heavy Again

When you have added the light guidelines for everything you want to include in the sketch, grab your soft pencil and make the lines bold and sure. Put in wallpaper pattern or wood lines (a little of this goes a long way), furniture, lamps, and rugs. Don't line up the furniture against the walls, but put appropriate pieces such as a sofa and chair out into the room, which will make the set more interesting to the camera and will give more opportunities for actor action.

To give your drawing some freehand character, do not put it on the floor and walk on it. Use your convenient thumb to smudge some of the lines and use the side of the pencil lead to create shadows. Some careless abandon at this point will take away the tight wiry look that mechanically produced sketches can have. It will also make the producer certain that he has hired a talented person.

GET SOME ROUGH COSTS

The producer will want to know how much the set will cost. You, the designer, need to stay within the budget. As you may not have much cost experience as a guide, how do you get a rough idea of the construction cost to present to the producer and director?

Later, after the construction drawings are finished, you will take the construction drawings with specific information to construction shops to get firm bids. For now, though, take your uncolored tracing-paper sketch to a couple of construction shops and ask them to give you a quick "ballpark" estimate. Most shops are glad to do so as you will probably ask them for a bid on the construction when that time comes. The basis for their rough cost estimate is based on dollars per running foot of flat wall and how much detailing they see in the sketch. Their bid does not include any set dressing, so you will need to visit a couple of property-rental houses with a list of the furniture and set dressings to get another rough estimate of these costs. If you find that the estimates exceed the budget figure you have been given, you can eliminate some set elements such as fancy door moldings, an entrance platform, or the breakfast bar. The construction shop supervisor can tell you how to bring the cost down within your budget. Also, ask the construction supervisor to give you a separate cost for setup on the stage.

Unless, by some miracle, the set is estimated to cost less than the budget allows, go ahead and make the changes on your tracing paper sketch.

No Coloring Yet

Stifle the urge to color the original sketch. Always preserve the original pencil-and-tracing-paper drawing. Take your sketch to a blueprint service and get some black line prints. Prints are priced by the square foot and are not expensive, so get a couple of extra ones as insurance against the chance you might spill something. If you think your sketch will look better reversed right to left, ask the printer to flop it for you. This will also make any lettering come out backward, so do it only with nonlettered sketches. You will be thrilled to see how much the blueprinting process enhances your sketch. Trim and mount a print on mat board with spray glue, rubber cement, or dry-mount tissue. *Now* go ahead and color with pencils or markers. Water-based paint may make the print wrinkle.

What Colors?

Have a color plan in mind. If you just start coloring the walls and furnishings with whatever pencil is at hand, the result will be confusing to the eye as well as to the camera. Decide what general color impression the set will give. It may be basically gray, brown, or whatever color suits the story and characters. Unless the set needs to be very colorful, grayed-down neutral wall colors and patterns provide a solid visual foundation in front of and on which to place the furniture and decorative objects. Bright colors work well in a neutral-colored environment. If wallpaper is appropriate on a wall of the set, choose a design that has three or four colors and achieve a color-coordinated look by repeating these colors in the upholstery, paint, and accessories. If you need to make copies of the color sketch, color laser copy machines can reproduce it accurately and can print other sizes as well.

THE TOUR BUS IS LEAVING

Sketch presentation usually causes some butterflies in the stomach, but if you have done your homework, carefully analyzed the problem, and accurately estimated the costs, just wait and see what happens. Give a guided tour around the drawing and point out camera angles that may not be apparent to the untrained eye. Chances are, your worst fears will not be realized and you will not have to slink from the room with your sketch under your arm. Be willing to listen to criticism and profit by it. You may have overlooked something.

When the sketch has impressed one and all, it's time to convert this representation into detailed construction drawings that will tell the carpenters how to translate the sketch into wood, metal, and paint. To make the construction drawings you will need a few more tools, which you will find out about in Chapter 11.

11

EQUIPMENT FOR CONSTRUCTION DRAWINGS

The producer and director think the sketches look totally inspired and have told you to go ahead with the project. What now? Do you just take the sketches to a carpenter shop and tell them to build it? No. Sets are built from sketches when time is short and an experienced set builder is available, but we are not going to work that way, taking what seems to be the easy way out. We are going to do it the right way, which is by making construction drawings and getting bids on the construction. To do this, however, you will need the following basic equipment: a drawing board, tracing paper, T square, architect's scale, triangles, 2H and 4H pencils, eraser, drafting tape, and a pencil sharpener. Art supply stores display an array of glittering gadgets as well to tempt the unwary artist. Most of this stuff is useful, but at the beginning it's best to start with simple tools. As your skill improves, get whatever additional tools you need and can afford.

YOUR DRAWING BOARD

A drawing board should be flat, have perfectly straight edges, and possess corners that form ninety-degree angles. Get the largest size you can accommodate. Boards smaller than 24" x 30" are not useful for making construction drawings. A good size is 30" x 40". It's not necessary to get a board with legs or a pedestal. The kitchen table has legs; you can devise a way to secure the board at a slant and still be able to take it wherever you need to work. Be kind to that piece of wood. Don't cut on it, throw knives at it, or stick pins in it. Later you may want to invest in a drawing table that has an adjustable slant top and built-in drawers. For the time being, however, a small chest of drawers works very well.

PAPER AND PENCILS FOR DRAFTING

Unlike sketches done freely with soft pencils, construction drawings require accurate lines drawn by harder pencil leads on better quality tracing paper. To help you choose, here are some suggestions.

Tracing Paper

Just to refresh your memory, the best way to go is with the roll. Buy good-quality paper for finished construction drawings, but use less-expensive paper for preliminary drawings, unless you expect to do an extraordinary amount of erasing. Art-supply stores sell drawing sheets with printed borders and title blocks. These sheets look impressive but force you to work within the confines of the borders. If you are sure that you can plan ahead far enough to use this type of paper, go ahead and invest in it. Tracing paper is also available with a grid of 1/8" and 1/4" squares printed in light blue that do not show on blueprints. This type of paper is useful when your T square, drawing board, and triangles are not available, as you can use any straightedge to draw horizontal and vertical lines in either of the two scales.

Pencils

If we used ink, fiber-tipped, or ballpoint pens to make construction drawings, they would be impossible to change. Pencil lines are easy to control and erase.

Everyone has favorites. Old art directors at The Home for Old Art Directors while away many hours in their rockers arguing the pros and cons of the lead pencil, the lead holder, and the mechanical pencil. Some like to use only one lead hardness and, by bearing down with more or less pressure, get various line weights. Others have pockets bristling with lead holders and mechanical pencils with many different lead hardnesses.

Wood-bodied lead pencils are the cheapest to buy but require constant sharpening and replacement. As the pencil gets shorter, it can be inserted in a pencil extender to squeeze the last bit of use out of it. An electric sharpener is very convenient for this type of pencil.

Metal lead holders use the same thickness of lead as the wood pencils but require only replacement of the leads inserted in the holder. The leads can be sharpened on sandpaper or with an electric lead sharpener.

Mechanical pencils use thin 0.5- or 0.7-millimeter leads that never need to be sharpened, remaining the same width as they are used. As the lead wears down, a push on the top of the holder propels more lead out of the tip.

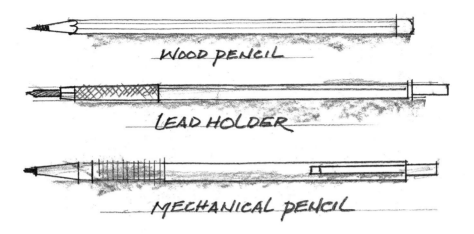

WOOD PENCIL

LEAD HOLDER

MECHANICAL PENCIL

Whatever type of pencil you get, start with two lead hardnesses: 2H for heavy lines and 4H for the light lines. Try different types of pencils and see which one calls out to you.

What If You Make a Mistake?

Erasers such as the Pink Pearl work fine for sketching as well as for construction drawings. If you plan to do a lot of erasing and hate to throw a drawing in the wastebasket, get an electric eraser. This may make everyone think you are an old pro or make them wonder if you make a lot of mistakes.

TOOLS

As guides for drawing accurate pencil lines on tracing paper, the T square, architect's scale, and triangle—along with the straight edge of the drawing board—work best.

The T Square

A T square allows one to draw horizontal lines that are parallel to each other and serves as the base for triangles, which allow you to draw perfectly vertical lines to the parallel ones or lines at angles. For construction drawings, a plain wood square with transparent plastic edges is just fine. Get a square the length of the long edge of your drawing board. Buy the best quality you can afford, but avoid fancy versions such as the clear acrylic

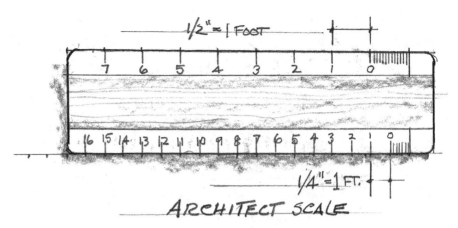

models. They look great but do not perform as well as the standard model with the AM radio and black-wall tires.

People who do a lot of drafting frequently use a drafting machine, which combines the functions of a T square, adjustable triangle, and architect's scale. This is not a machine that does the drafting for you but is an arrangement of counterbalanced metal rods, arranged like the human arm, that clamps to the top of the drawing board. The end of the arm that rests on the drawing surface holds an adjustable knob that has two transparent architect's scales at a ninety-degree angle to each other. When the arm tension is adjusted properly, the knob and scales can be moved anywhere on the drawing surface and will remain in place, even when the drawing board is in a vertical position. The position of the scale edges can be set at any angle.

T Square Don'ts

Don't

> Use it for a hammer
> Cut along its edges
> Allow it to fall on its head
> Let it get wet
> Leave it in the sun
> Let kids play with it
> Loan it to anyone

The Scale of an Architect

If we were to make drawings in 1' = 1' scale, the drawings would be too huge to handle, so an architect's scale is most useful. With the aid of an architect's scale, you can convert full-size feet-and-inch measurements into

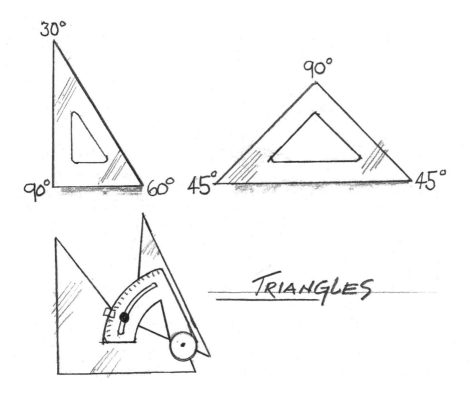

30°

90°

90°   60°   45°   45°

TRIANGLES

smaller units that represent feet and inches. Be sure to get an architect's scale, not an engineer's scale.

Scales come in several shapes and sizes. A popular kind is the triangular shape that has two measurement systems on each edge. Flat scales have two scale measurements on each edge. The short flat scales are easy to carry in your pocket and make you look very professional. Most construction drawing for television and motion picture use is done in 1/4" = 1' or 1/2" = 1' scale. The same don'ts apply to the scales as listed for T squares, plus a couple of others: don't draw lines against the edges (use your T square or triangles) or throw it across the room when things go wrong.

Triangles

These fascinating pieces of transparent plastic have three perfectly straight edges placed at different angles to each other. When placed on the paper with one of the edges against the T square edge, the triangle allows you to draw perpendicular lines as well as lines at angles. A 30–60-degree triangle has one corner that measures 90 degrees, one that is 60 degrees and one at 30 degrees. If you were paying attention in geometry class, you will realize how many possibilities are inherent in the lowly triangle. If you were paying attention while reading the preceding words, you understand what a

45–45-degree triangle does. Even more exciting is the *adjustable triangle!* It allows you to draw any angle you please with just one instrument.

Buy the best-quality tools and materials you can afford. Good equipment lasts longer than poorly made stuff and is a pleasure to use.

YOUR WORK AREA

Now you need a place in which to work. This does not mean that you need a big studio with skylights. Dream about that for the future. The corner of a room with some available space for a drawing board, a stool, and a small chest of drawers can work. Available daylight is nice, but provide a flexible lamp for those times when work is due the next morning and you have to stay up all night.

Now, about the drawing board. As pointed out earlier, it's not necessary to spend a lot of money on a gorgeous pedestal type. A 30-inch-by-40-inch plain-wood hollow-core board works just fine. The lumberyard stocks hollow slab doors and plywood sheets in many sizes and surfaces, as well as metal or wood legs. Finish the wood with your choice of stain, wax, or paint. Roll white vinyl sheeting glued to the wood surface is easy to keep clean and provides a resilient drawing surface. Art supply stores stock cushioned plastic sheets for surfacing drawing boards. What holds it up? If your room space is limited, you can hinge the surface to the wall and let it hang down against the wall when not in use. Open wood boxes or plastic milk crates stacked on top of each other are another base possibility. These provide storage space for books and supplies as well as holding up your work surface. Make these elements stable by fastening them together securely. A wiggly drawing board is about as bad as none at all.

Most designers like to sit on a stool. This way you can look down on your work and can get up and down easily when the mood to pace strikes. To slant your drawing board as it sits on the slab surface, a couple of triangular pieces of wood or small blocks under the board will work.

The top of your storage chest should be at a comfortable height for reaching for drawing tools. While an open shelf unit provides easy access to drawing instruments, the shelves and equipment collect dust.

COMPUTER-AIDED DRAFTING (CAD)

At this time, CAD has not proven to be particularly useful in television and film work. For a freelance art director, the hardware and software are expensive and take time to acquire proficiency.

A basic CAD system requires a computer with at least 640 kilobytes of random-access memory and an 80386 processor, a 20-megabyte or larger hard disk, a VGA monitor, a mouse, and a plotter that prints the drawings, as well as the application software that tells the computer what to do. With a system such as this, one can produce plans, elevations, and three-dimensional shaded renderings. Using a modem, the computer can send the drawings over telephone lines or a satellite system to another computer capable of receiving them. Some architectural firms find CAD systems useful for communicating visually with branch offices and for producing perspective views of proposed structures for clients.

Computers are good at doing calculations, manipulating data, and cranking out repetitive work, none of which are major concerns in the type of work we do, which is usually one-of-a-kind drawings. Art directors on continuously running shows such as daytime dramas and game shows that require daily changes can make use of computer-aided drafting equipment, but few freelancers have found it to be very practical.

If you do not already own computer equipment such as that described above and want to consider using CAD, go to several reputable computer software outlets and talk to knowledgeable salespeople. Tell them you want to see and learn about computer-aided drafting packages. Among other packages, TURBOCAD from International Software is an excellent choice.

Ask to see the instruction manual that comes with each package. The manual outlines what the software can do, specifies what hardware is needed to run it, and usually provides a tutorial to guide you through the learning process. Remember that drawing with a computer is very different from using paper and pencil; it takes time and effort to get comfortable with it.

Ask Some Questions

- What equipment do I need to run the software?
- Will the software work with a plotter that produces large-sheet drawings and with a personal computer printer that prints a maximum size of 8 1/2" x 14"?
- Can I make perspective drawings?
- Will the software measure and add dimensions to plans?
- Can I use different drawing scales?
- Will the application convert to the metric system?
- Is there a library of standard units such as doors, windows, and furniture?
- Can I return the software if I don't like it?

After deciding on the right CAD software for you, take your list of requirements to several computer hardware outlets and shop for the best price. Some stores offer discounts for all-at-once purchases. Be sure the computer you buy can accommodate future additions, such as a CD ROM (digital disk library) drive, expanded memory, or a larger hard disk.

If you have little or no computer experience but feel that CAD will be helpful now and in the future, be patient while learning. Get comfortable with the equipment. The manuals do not tell you everything; you have to use your reasoning powers too.

With sketches in hand and all that professional-looking drafting equipment staring at us, let's go on to the next chapter and begin some construction drawings.

THE CONSTRUCTION DRAWING

Now that you have done the research, the sketches have been praised and approved by the producer and director, and you have your drawing board and basic equipment ready, the next step is to translate the sketches into specific working drawings for carpenters.

First, let's look at three different types of drafting: engineering, architectural, and film and video. Engineering and architectural drafting require precise detail, as the final product has to last a long time and the parts must fit together with close tolerances. Film and video drafting, however, uses many standard units such as flats, platforms, and backings; it displays surfaces more than internal structure. Architects and engineers are usually horrified to see what appears to be a rough sketch on a set construction print, but such a print is adequate and standard to a set construction carpenter.

This is not to say that our construction drawings should be sloppy, but they should include only as much precision and detail as is necessary, based on standard set construction methods. For example, we don't need to draw the back of a normal set piece because experienced set carpenters know how they should look.

To estimate accurately the cost of building sets, shops need to have specific information on what materials they will need and what dimensions are required, so they can accurately compute material and labor costs. If you are working for an independent producer who does not have studio facilities at his disposal, you will need to print several sets of the construction drawings to take to construction shops and get bids to compare on the set construction.

If you are working at a studio that has a construction shop, your drawings will come under the scrutiny of an estimator who will determine how much the set will cost to build. If you have designed sets that exceed the show budget, you will have to simplify the sets by cutting down on the detailing or by reducing the size and number of sets, conferring with the producer or production manager.

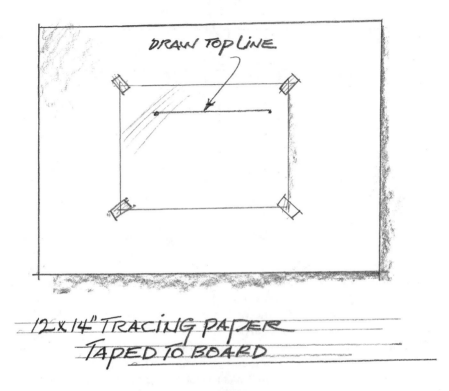

12 x 14" TRACING PAPER TAPED TO BOARD

WHAT'S THE PLAN?

Begin by drawing a temporary *plan view* of Patty's living room. This will be a view of the room from the top with no perspective. Look at your sketch of Patty's living room and determine how wide the back (upstage) wall should be. Remember that sets look somewhat larger on camera than they do to the eye. Measure a familiar room for comparison.

Tracing Paper Again

Tear off a piece of tracing paper about 12" x 14" and tape it to your drawing board with the 12" dimension vertical. With the T square head snugly against the left edge of the drawing board (if you draw with your right hand), slide the square into place and draw a *light* line across the paper about two inches from the top. With the 1/2" = 1' side of the architect's scale on the light line you have drawn, make a dot on the line at the zero feet mark and another dot at the number that you have decided will be the width in feet of the back wall of Patty's living room. Do not draw against the scale edge, as it will become very dirty and hard to read.

Put the scale aside, and with T square and pencil draw a heavier line from dot to dot on the light line. This line represents the width of the back

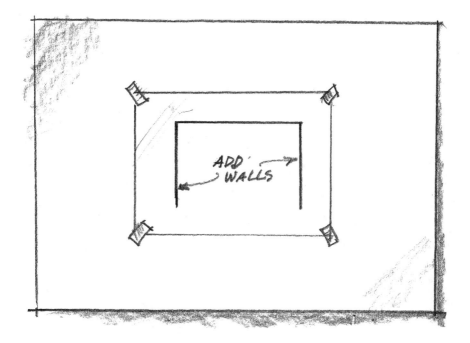

wall of Patty's living room. Standard practice is to work from left to right. Draw the left wall, which meets the back wall at a 90-degree angle. Slide the T square down the paper and place the short straightedge of the transparent triangle on the paper and against the edge of the T square. Slide the vertical edge of the triangle to where it meets the left end of the back wall and draw a light vertical line.

Determine how wide the wall that comes out toward the camera should be, and with the aid of the architect's scale make a dot where the wall ends. If this looks right, draw a heavier line to indicate this wall. Proceed around the three walls of the set in this way, drawing in the walls with just one heavy line, until you have completed what you think is the necessary size for this set. The set walls you have just drawn should look like an upside-down **U**.

Indicate some major pieces of furniture if you want, just to get an idea of how these pieces will fit in the set, but don't include them on the construction drawings unless they are built-ins or affect the construction of the walls. Remember that furniture must be drawn in the same scale as the walls. Art supply stores have furniture templates that have shapes representing typically sized tables, chairs, sofas, etc., cut out as holes in transparent plastic.

You have now finished the temporary plan view of Patty's living room, but without any dimension lines, which you will add later. For now, leave the drawing this simple, as you will add detailing such as windows, doors, etc., later.

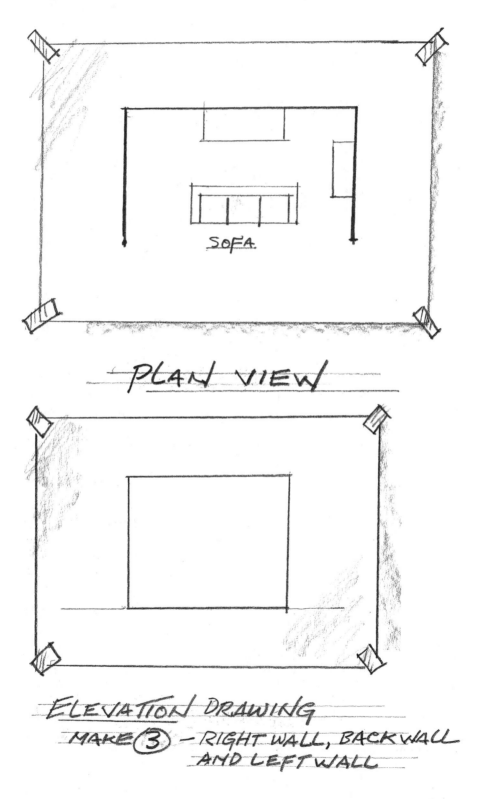

PLAN VIEW

SOFA

ELEVATION DRAWING
MAKE ③ — RIGHT WALL, BACK WALL
AND LEFT WALL

THE ELEVATIONS

The *plan view* shows how the set will look from the top, as though you are looking down from the ceiling. Now you need to show how the set will look to the camera when it looks directly at each of the three walls with no perspective shown.

The next three drawings are *elevations.* Put the plan view drawing aside and tear off three pieces of tracing paper, each wide enough to contain a drawing of the camera left wall, the upstage wall, and the camera right wall.

Tape one piece of tracing paper to your drawing board and draw a light line an inch from the bottom. This drawing will represent the bottom of the camera left wall of Patty's living room. Using the dot, light line, and architect's scale method, measure off the width of the wall and draw a heavy line on the light guideline.

Check the length of this line with the line on the plan view to make sure they are the same length. Do this with each width line to make sure they match the plan view. Place the 90-degree edge of the triangle vertically on the T square edge and draw a vertical line the height of the wall toward the left edge of the paper. This represents the left edge of the wall as you face it. Continue to draw the wall outlines and draw in doors and windows with heavy lines.

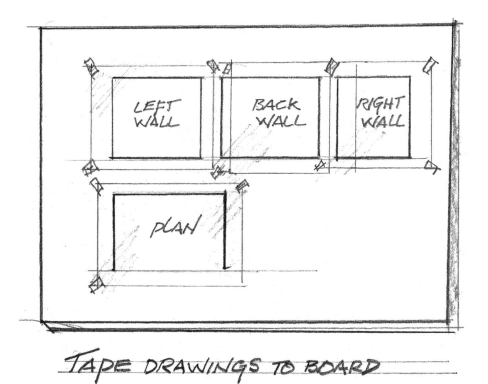

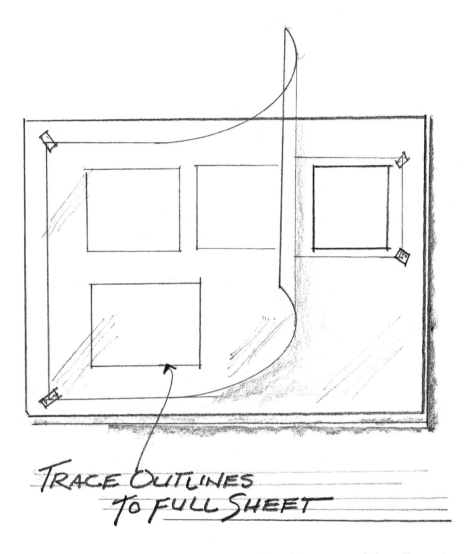

Trace Outlines to Full Sheet

When you have finished this *elevation view* of the camera left wall, put it aside and make outline drawings of the upstage and right walls. Delay putting in such details as picture moldings, chair rails, and dimension lines. Do that in the next step, which will be the full-sheet drawings. These three elevation drawings are size and outline guides to place under the large sheet of tracing paper that will be drawing sheet No. 1.

The Next Step

Tape the three *elevation drawings* about two inches apart on your drawing board. Line them up with the T square so that the tops and bottoms line up and the vertical lines are parallel to each other.

Tape the plan view three or four inches below the camera left wall draw-ing. Line up the left side of the plan view drawing with the left side of the left wall drawing. Now, tear off a piece of tracing paper large enough to cover the four drawings with six inches of space all the way around. Center it over the four drawings and tape it at the corners. At the bottom of the wall elevation drawings, draw a light guideline for some lettering later.

Make sure that the bottoms of the elevation drawings line up with this line. If they don't, loosen two corners of the large sheet and adjust the posi-tions of the temporary drawings. Trace the outlines of the three walls and the plan view to the large sheet. Leave paper space reserved for other infor-mation around the outside of the main drawing area.

Once you have become more familiar with this type of construction drawing, you may want to plunge right ahead to the full-sheet drawing that is coming up, but for now, keeping the plan and elevation drawings on separate pieces of tracing paper is the best way to go.

Next, we will see how to add the all-important dimension lines, detailing, labels, and descriptive information.

13

FINISHING THE CONSTRUCTION DRAWINGS

One of the most satisfying aspects of the art director's job is to see the finished sets standing on the stage, nicely dressed and lit. Before this can happen, though, we have to finish the drawings and supervise construction, setup, and dressing.

What you should have now is a row of three elevation drawings of Patty's living room at the top of your large sheet of tracing paper, and a plan view of the room at the lower left with a generous amount of blank space around the edges of the paper.

TRANSFERRING THE DRAWINGS

Remove the individual drawings from under the large piece of tracing paper, because you have traced their major outlines to the large sheet. Save the individual drawings, just in case. During the tracing process, some of the pencil lines from the surfaces of the individual drawings may have

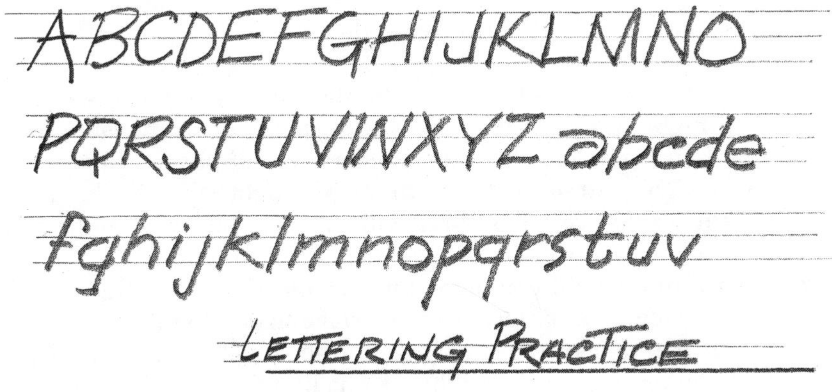

ABCDEFGHIJKLMNO

PQRSTUVWXYZ abcde

fghijklmnopqrstuv

LETTERING PRACTICE

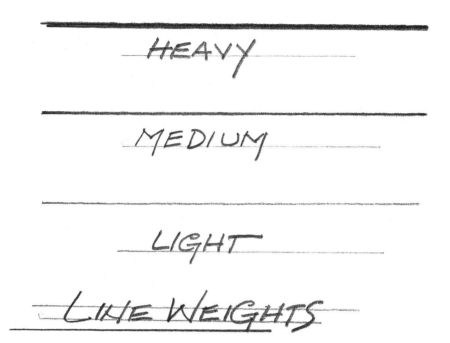

transferred themselves to the back of the large sheet. Turn the large sheet over, erase the unwanted lines, and tape the sheet back to the drawing board.

Lettering

Make your lettering easy to read. Practice by drawing three light guidelines on a piece of paper and fill three or four practice sheets. If you have a lot of difficulty at first, buy a lettering template. As your skill improves, you will develop your own lettering style.

Line Weights

We will use three weights of lines: *heavy* for the outlines of the flats, *medium* for the lettering and stage floor line, and *light* for the dimension lines. Practice drawing these three lines on another piece of paper and squint at them to see if they read as heavy, medium, and light when held at arm's length. Remember that very light lines will not reproduce well in the blue-printing process.

Draw a medium-weight continuous line across the bottom lines of the three elevation views. Letter just below it "stage floor," to indicate that the flats stand on the floor of the stage and are not suspended above. Begin drawing *dimension lines* with a light-weight line. You have some space

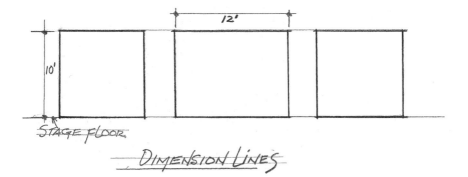

between the three elevation drawings of the room walls for the dimension lines. Beginning at the left wall of the elevation drawings, draw a dimension line about half an inch away from the heavier edge line of the flat. If you draw the dimension lines too close to the flat outline, there won't be room for the numbers indicating the heights of the flats.

Dimension Lines

The vertical dimension lines go from the stage floor line to the top line of the flats where you drew the light guideline. With the T square, draw a horizontal line from the top of the flat where it crosses the vertical dimension line you just drew. At the point where they cross, make a heavy dot or a little slash mark to indicate that the dimension line stops there. When drawing dimension lines, let them not quite touch the flat outline, so there is no question that they are dimension lines rather than outlines. Put in the numbers that indicate height or width. The numbers go between the wall edge line and the dimension line, but closer to the dimension line. Print the numbers *clearly* with a medium-weight pencil so that they pop out from the dimension lines and are easy to read.

Draw the horizontal dimensions of the flats the same way you drew the vertical ones. Use the space you left at the top of the paper to show the width of the flats. The space below the stage floor line is reserved for other information to be added later. Remember to leave enough space between the dimension lines and the flat outlines for the numbers. Be sure the dimension lines are clearly lighter than the flat-outline lines, and that the dimension lines do not connect with, but end just short of, the flat outlines. When you have finished adding the major dimension lines, stand back from the drawing and squint at it. Do the shapes of the flats stand out clearly? If they don't, go back in there and make the outlines heavier. Be sure there is plenty of contrast between the dimension lines and the flat outlines. Otherwise, the carpenters may begin building dimension lines.

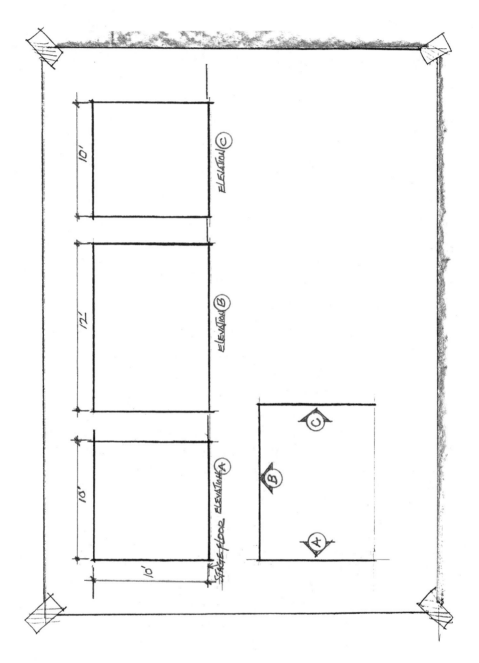

LABELING

The next step is to *label* the plan and elevation drawings. About an inch below the stage floor line, draw light guidelines below the row of elevation drawings. On this line and centered below each of three wall flats, draw a 1/2″-diameter circle with a template or compass. On the plan drawing,

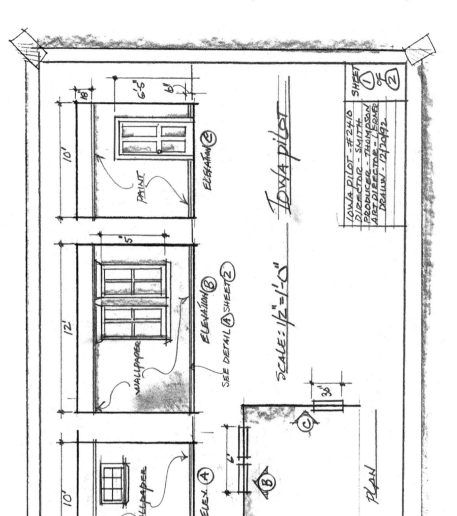

draw the same size circle about an inch away from each of the three walls on the inside of the drawing. At the edge of each of these circles, draw a 90-degree angle with the corner of a triangle, so that it touches the edge of the circle as an arrow point that will point at each wall surface on the plan. Beginning at the left wall elevation, draw the letter A in the center of the circle, B in the next one, and so on. When you have A, B, and C lettered on the wall elevations, go to the plan drawing and put the letters that corre-spond to the wall elevation views in the circle-arrows that are in front of each wall. Make these letters bold so that they pop out of the sheet and are easy to see. Now that the views are labeled, anyone who looks at the plan view can tell which line represents which wall in the elevation drawings and vice versa.

LOOK AT THE DETAILS

When you look at the elevation drawings, do the surfaces look flat and uninteresting? Possibly so, as we have been working with general shapes and surfaces and have not added elements that give the walls a realistic sculptural look, such as paneled doors, door frame moldings, baseboards, light switches, and heating vents. A long, unbroken wall surface can profit from the addition of a jog, corner, or structural pillars. When using several stock (already-built) flats to make up a wall, instead of taping and painting a joint, indicate a one-foot-wide flat on the surface to cover the joint. The taped and painted joints on both sides of the added flat will not be as noticeable as they would be on a flat surface. Specify textured paint, which will give added interest to flat surfaces.

Detail drawings of complex moldings or other architectural features are indicated by lettering "DETAIL (A)" or "(B)," etc., at the point where they occur on the plan or elevation drawing. Place a larger-scale drawing of the detail on the construction drawing where there is some unused space. If the construction drawings need many detail drawings for which there is no room on the sheet, label the details "DETAIL (A)—SHEET (12)" or consecu-tive letters and create a separate sheet for the detail drawings.

Aging

If the room needs to have a worn look, indicate light, medium, or heavy *aging* as a note on the drawings. To the carpenters, this will mean that they can create nicks and worn-looking surfaces on the doors and walls. Scenic artists can apply thin washes to the wall surfaces and fog darker colors in the set corners to age the set.

Label the Surfaces

By looking at the drawing so far, the viewer knows what the heights and widths of the flats are, but not what the surface treatments are. If a surface is wallpaper, draw a couple of light lettering guidelines near the center of the elevation drawing of the flat and letter in "WALLPAPER." Draw a sinu-ous line off the center of the word to the top of the wallpaper surface and do the same off the bottom of the lettering. If you are sure of the wallpaper number at this time, put that in, too. Do the same lettering job with each surface, whatever it may be. For bricks, stone, or wood, draw an indication of them on a portion of the flat.

Finishing Touches

Boldly letter the word "PLAN" below the plan view and the word "ELE-VATION" at the left of each circle-arrow indicating that it identifies an elevation or plan view.

Lettering

Letter "SCALE: 1/2" = 1'-0'" (or whatever scale you are using) in bold letters near the bottom of the sheet. Draw a heavy border line around the edges of the sheet about an inch from the edges of the drawing area. If you have lots of extra blank paper around the outside, just trim or tear it off an inch outside the border lines. At the lower right corner of the border, draw a *title block* that will be about three inches high and five inches wide with lines containing some basic information: production title and number, set name and number, producer, director, art director, shooting dates, scale of drawing, date of drawing, approved by, budget number, sheet number, drawn by, and total number of sheets.

PRINTING THE DRAWING SHEET

Before having the drawings blueprinted, go over the drawings with the director, producer, and anyone else concerned with the set. Remember that many people have trouble interpreting construction drawings, so have the set sketch at hand to help explain the construction drawings. Give your audience a detailed explanation of each sheet to help them understand what you have in mind. After each of these groups has reviewed the prints, make any necessary changes on the drawings and have sets of blueprints made. Drawings are done in pencil because changes are easy to make by erasing and redrawing.

How to Print the Drawings

Blueprinting is the traditional practical way to duplicate drawings done on tracing paper. The drawing done in pencil on tracing paper runs through a machine in which light shines through it onto sensitized paper. Very light lines do not print well, necessitating overexposing the print, which will produce a lot of confusing background texture. Lines should be firm and clear on the original drawing.

The blueprinter can print drawings on paper in black, blue, or brown lines. The first set can be printed in black, and after you have made changes, the next printed in blue lines, to help distinguish between progressive sets of prints. If you do not want to change your original tracing-paper drawing, the printer can also produce a brown-line copy on translucent paper, from which you can chemically erase lines, draw new ones, and have prints made. A common practice to call attention to changes on progressive sets of prints is to draw a bold hollow arrow marked "CHANGE (DATE)" pointing at the concerned area.

Our exercise requires only one drawing sheet, but in the case of more sheets necessary to depict all the sets, put a large sheet number in the lower right corner of the title block and indicate the total number of sheets so that it's easy to see if all the sheets are there. A typical distribution list for sets of construction drawings is as follows: construction head, producer, director, production manager, crew chief, lighting director, technical director, art director, assistant director, prop master, and stage manager.

The construction shop should have more than one set and so should the art director. Other members of the company can have more sets as requested. The more key people who know what the set is going to look like, the better off the production will be and the fewer headaches the art director will have. The art director prepares a set of elevation and plan prints with color chip samples, furniture indications, and set dressing information for the set decorator.

Now that the construction drawings are finished, we can easily make a simple model of the set, using prints of the drawings. The next chapter will show how to do this.

14

MODEL MAKING

Models communicate spaces, sizes, and shapes to anyone who gazes upon them. A model helps the art director see the set more clearly and make changes that can be expensive once the sets are built. Directors use models to see camera angles. If the art director has to sell a design to a producer to get the job, a model can do the trick.

DIFFERENT TYPES OF MODELS

Models made to depict settings for use in the theater are usually more detailed than those made for motion pictures and television. A theatrical model may even have a miniature lighting system built into it so that the effect of lighting changes can be seen. Unless the theater piece is to be seen in the round, the theatrical set model includes the proscenium, or frame that defines the limits of the set the audience will see. As the television or motion picture setting's frame is the camera view, the models for these mediums do not have prosceniums, of course, but present the set as it will look to the camera, with the possibility of many different angles.

The Big White Set

This exercise model will be a *white model*: no color. Its purpose will be to show the scale of the walls, the proportions of the spaces, and the location of openings. If you are sure that you want to make a color model, add the color before you glue the pieces in place on the base.

You Have to Carry It Around

What scale should the model be? If the set is large and the model will be cumbersome to carry, stick to 1/4" = 1'. If you determine that the finished model will be a manageable size if you use 1″ = 1′, then do that. If you can make the model to the same scale as the elevation drawings, your job will be easier, as you will see. If you use a different scale for the model than you used for the blueprints, you will have to measure out each piece of the model in a different scale.

MATERIALS FOR MODEL MAKING

Plan and elevation blueprints
Drawing board on which a cutting surface can be taped
Metal T square
Metal triangle
Soft and hard pencils
Drafting tape
Cutting knife such as X-Acto
Mat board, tag board, or plastic foam–based board
Base material on which to place the model
Glue of your choice
Pins—Glass headed and pushpins
Wood—Balsa strips and flat sheets
Paint, Colored pencils, markers (if you want to color the model)

START WITH A SOUND BASE

A good material to use is foam-based board, which is a sandwich of two layers of paper or plastic with a core of plastic foam. This material is light, rigid, strong, and comes in many thicknesses. Use the thin weights for walls, architectural details, and furniture. Other materials for walls and platforms that work well are mat board, two-ply Strathmore paper, tag board, and balsawood sheets. All these materials are easy to cut with a mat knife.

Start Slicing

Cut a piece of base material to size, cutting against the edge of a metal T square or metal straightedge. Do not cut against the edge of plastic or wood-edged drawing tools. Always cut away from your body. Leave about two inches of space around the outside of the area the model will occupy to provide space for labeling.

A Quick Way to Make the Model

If you are going to use the same scale in the model as you used for the working drawings, get a black line print made of the elevation drawings.

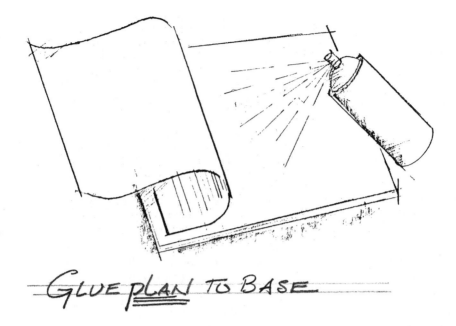

GLUE pLAN TO BASE

Use spray glue or rubber cement to adhere the elevation and plan views to a piece of the thin foam board, cardboard, or balsa wood you have decided to use for the model set walls. If you use 1/4" or thicker board for the walls, the corners will be difficult to make.

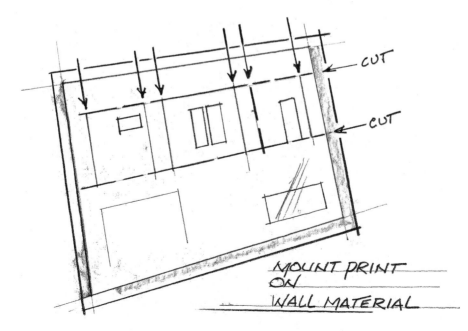

CUT

CUT

MOUNT PRINT
ON
WALL MATERIAL

THE SET MODEL WALLS

Tape the mounted print to a surface on which you can cut. Using a *metal* T square edge, against which you will cut, line it up with the horizontal lines of the elevation drawings and make long cuts across the top and bottom of the group. Then, with a *metal* triangle placed against the edge of the T square, cut the vertical lines of the walls. You can also, at this time, make bend cuts at the vertical lines where you need to make a corner. If you cut all the way through, you will have to glue or tape the walls together later, but if you cut only partway through and bend the corner at that point, you will save some time and have a neater corner.

While you have the mounted plan and elevation views taped to the cutting surface, cut partway through the vertical lines where the walls make a corner going away from the camera. Where a corner makes the wall turn toward the camera, make a little tick mark at the top and bottom of the corner walls while the piece is face up so that you can tell where the top and bottom of the flat are when you turn the piece over and cut on the back. Make the cut partway through the back of the material, and bend the wall toward the camera. Cut the door and window openings. Cut partway through the material on the hinged side of the door so that the door can be bent open to show the direction of the door swing.

NOW WE'RE GETTING SOMEWHERE

The next step is to mount the plan view from the print on the model base. Spray glue or rubber cement works well. Water-based glues will make the print wrinkle. Center the plan view and trim the edges to the edge of the model base. Lightly tape the model flats to the plan with drafting tape at a few points on the back of the flats. If all is well, and the pieces fit on the plan view, glue them down at a few points. If you spread glue over the entire bottom of the flat pieces, they will be very difficult to remove if you need to change their position. If the set includes overhead beams or ceiling pieces, put them in at this time. If you have the time, add details such as balsa-strip window trim, moldings, furniture pieces, and other detailing. Some craft shops and dollhouse-supply stores have all kinds of furniture and household objects made to scale, as well as printed scale wallpaper. You can also make your own furniture and accessories from leftover wall scraps.

HUMAN SCALE

To help viewers visualize the size of the set, cut out a simple human figure at scale height and place it somewhere in the model. When you and your clients view the model, hold it up to eye level and rotate it as though the

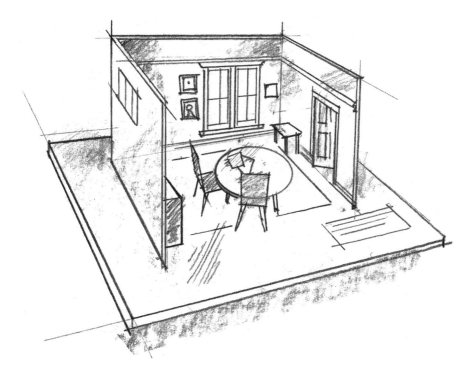

viewer's eye is the camera. This will let the model serve its purpose, which is to give an idea of possible camera angles, spaces, and proportions. Remember that the people to whom you will be showing the model have not seen it before, although you are familiar with all of its great qualities, as well as the blobs of glue you couldn't remove and hope no one will notice.

After discussing the model with the producer and director, you may need to make some changes. As the original plans and elevations are done in easily erasable pencil, erase and add to the original drawings, have some new prints made, and revise the model.

The art director has designed the sets, made sketches, distributed prints, and built a model. To see that construction and the stage setup goes as planned, the art director still has a lot of things to do, as you will see in the next chapter.

SUPERVISING
CONSTRUCTION AND SETUP

Now that the construction drawings and model are finished and approved, the art director finds a construction shop to build the sets, supervises the construction, and oversees the stage setup.

GETTING BIDS

If the studio the producer has selected has a construction shop, the sets may be built there. If not, the art director takes the drawings to several shops for bids. The lowest bid is not necessarily the best one, because a shop may want the job badly enough to cut corners, to the detriment of the job. To avoid unnecessary building of new units, the construction shop can use previously built flats or other stock units, which saves time and money. Major production centers have independent rental facilities that stock pieces of existing sets such as basic flats, fireplaces, and door and window units that can be rented for the production and returned to stock later. The art director decides if the rental, transportation, and refinishing costs are less than building new pieces. Besides price, familiarity with the quality of work done by different shops is a deciding factor in construction shop choices.

CONSTRUCTION SUPERVISION

During set construction, the art director or an assistant should be available by beeper, answering machine, call forwarding, or answering service. Also, a 7:00 A.M. consultation at the construction shop each day can save time, money, and later anguish.

SETUP SUPERVISION

The production plan will allow a specified amount of time to install the sets on the stage, depending on the complexity of the sets. The art director is present at this time to see that the sets are placed according to the provided stage plan as discussed with the director. Do the walls fit together properly? Are details such as moldings, chair rails, and ceiling pieces placed and finished according to the blueprints? Have the scenic artists and set painters followed the paint plan and color samples accurately?

The art director or production designer is usually contracted for the duration of the production, including disposal of the sets. In some cases, though, the art director is released after the director and producer approve the sets as they stand on the stage. Whichever the agreement, the art director supervises the stage setup, set decoration, prop selection, scenic art, and special effects.

SET DECORATION

The set decorator, working with the plans provided by the art director, locates, rents, and purchases furniture, drapery, and decorative properties. The set decorator prepares a cost sheet, based on the set sketches and construction drawings, and keeps a running account of costs.

Set decorators working on location sometimes have properties shipped to the location from a major production center if appropriate pieces are not

available near the location. If it is possible to locate necessary objects locally, the decorator then rents or borrows them. Larger production centers have many prop (property) houses that rent furniture, decorative accessories, and specialized objects in many periods and styles. The set decorator, after studying the script and consulting the art director, roams the halls of these fascinating places and selects objects that are rented for the duration of the production. The rental charge averages about fifteen percent of the assigned value of the piece per week. Unless the production company sets up an account with the prop house, the house can require a cashier's check or cash deposit equal to the value of each piece and another check or cash deposit equal to the rental charge. When the rented props are returned in good condition, the deposit check is returned. If the set decorator wishes to paint or alter rented objects, permission to do so is required by the prop house. If the production runs for a long time, prop houses will work out a production rental plan, which costs less than weekly rental.

The set decorator keeps a photographic record of the set. As the set stands from day to day, furniture and other objects must remain in the same places so that shots will match and furniture will not appear to jump from one place to another from shot to shot. If a dinner scene, for example, is shot for several days, the set decorator takes Polaroid shots of the table after the last take of the day so that in case someone moves any of the objects on the table, the next day the set decorator can refer to the photographs and correct the table settings to match those of the previous day. Standard practice is to place a rope or other barrier across the set with a sign "Hot Set," which lets everyone know that the set is not to be disturbed.

The set decorator's photographs are extremely valuable if the set has been struck (dismantled) and needs to be reset for more photography matching the previous footage. An accident in the lab may have ruined the film, the story may have changed, or additional footage may be needed to clarify the story. An efficient set decorator keeps copies of the rental-house lists and can rerent furniture and decorative objects, arranging them to match the photographs. Sometimes, however, some of the objects are not available, so the decorator consults with the art director and director to shoot around certain pieces.

THE PROP MASTER

The prop master collects hand props such as beverages and other articles that are handled by the actors. If the set contains valuable pieces of silver or art, at the end of the day the prop master places marks on the supporting surfaces so that the objects can be replaced in exactly the same place the next day. The prop master then stores the pieces in a secure place and uses the marks and the Polaroid photographs to re-create the previous day's setup. Set painters and scenic artists paint the walls and woodwork and scenic artists apply finishes that require unusual skill, such as marbleizing floors and fireplaces. Some of this work is done in the construction shop to save time on the stage.

SPECIAL EFFECTS EXPERTS

The special-effects crew creates fire effects, fog, rain, running water, wind, or any other effects that require special electronic or mechanical action.

On a run-of-the-production contract, the art director will be available until the production wraps and for the disposal or storage of the sets. If the art director has an assistant, either of them is on the set or available at all times to take care of daily unforeseen changes. The art director may also have to work ahead of the production company shoot, preparing locations or new sets for the stage.

THE ART DIRECTOR'S CRITIQUE

So we see that the art director's job is not finished when the sets are designed. The art director takes a hard look at the sets when they are standing and lit, comparing the original concept with the reality. Sets always look a bit different from the original concept, but perhaps the living room was too large, as the director predicted, or our favorite, the nightclub, wasn't glitzy enough. Maybe the backing behind a window looks unconvincing; a little smoke generator between the set and the backing will diffuse and push back the painted scene, making it more realistic.

So far, we have seen the technical demands made on an art director: analyzing the script and characters, making sketches, doing construction drawings and models, and supervising the results in our sample project. Now, in Part III, we will see more of what the range of an art director's work is like on a practical, everyday basis.

PART III

TYPICAL SETS AND OPPORTUNITIES

A designer meets many different challenges. Part III details several typical ones: location work, a talk show, a news broadcasting environment, and a commercial, with emphasis on creating an innovative design.

For the novice considering a career in art direction, the last chapter offers suggestions on allied fields in which to gain applicable experience, as well as how to prepare a rèsumè and portfolio and where to look for a position in television and film.

16

AN ART DIRECTOR ON LOCATION

Leaving the convenience of the stage and working on location presents a different set of requirements for the art director as well as for the rest of the crew. The distance factor is a major consideration for the producer. A location may require minutes to days of travel and unknown and unpredictable factors can be expensive and time consuming.

IOWA MOVES TO ANOTHER STATE

A television network has provided the funds to the producer of the Iowa small-town project for one pilot episode to be recorded on videotape. The producer hopes that the network will be so enchanted with the result that the network will buy six more episodes, that the series will be a success, and that it will go into syndication after a many-year run.

The producer decides to tape all the interiors and the park scene on a soundstage and find a nearby small town that can be used, with some alterations, for exterior shooting. He does not feel that existing standing exterior sets on local motion picture back lots are convincing enough for the mood of the story as he and the director see it.

Marian Lerner, an art director who specializes in television video location work, has signed on as art director for the Iowa small-town project. She has a contract for six weeks' work and has received a check from the production company for one-third of her total fee, the other portions of which are scheduled to appear at two-week intervals. After presenting sketches, models, and construction drawings, Marian is ready to go on a location-survey trip.

Having already done research on Iowa small towns to design the sets, Marian has a good idea of the kind of town they will be looking for, so she obtains information on nearby small towns from the state motion picture office. Marian confers with the producer and production manager. They decide to look at two towns: Clarion and Two Forks. Both are in flat country and have some stores and houses of an adaptable style.

They rent a car and drive to Clarion. Marian observes the surrounding countryside. It is indeed flat, but a range of hills dominates the horizon. She sees that while the main street of Clarion has some older buildings, most of the structures have been altered to someone's idea of contemporary style. While the Iowa town they are depicting in the television series is not a backward-looking place or a historical monument, the survey group feels that the basically conservative attitude of the town elders in the series might have maintained the original style of the town's buildings.

Meet the Mayor

The group meets with the mayor of Clarion, who is eager to see the town star in a television series. He is sure it would be good for business. The producer makes it clear that other towns are being considered and that his decision will be based on many factors, even though Clarion is a fine place to consider.

Marian gets a street map of Clarion and takes many photographs of Main Street, individual buildings, the newspaper office, and residences. She places a yardstick, marked off at one-foot intervals with white tape, in each photograph so that if she needs to make scale drawings of any of the buildings, the size of the buildings will be apparent for scaling purposes.

Down the Road a Piece

The survey crew then drives a few miles down the road to look at Two Forks. They learn that while Two Forks is similar in appearance to Clarion, it does not have adequate lodging facilities for the cast and crew. Also, the main street features many palm trees growing in the center divider. If an aerial view is desired, the trees would be a problem, as well as in establishing shots. A matte process could be used to replace the upper part of the picture with the appropriate trees, but the producer will not be likely to spend the additional money for this effect.

As no other likely looking towns have presented themselves, the producer decides to use Two Forks for the location work. Marian does another analysis of the script based on the location choice. After conferences with the associate producer and production manager, Marian goes to Two Forks accompanied by George Wilson, the assistant art director who will be doing the revised construction drawings for the stage and location.

The producer has provided letters of agreement and contracts for the individual people and businesses involved in the Two Forks shoot. He has also obtained the necessary permits from City Hall, so that when the art director and her assistant visit the newspaper office and home owner, they are prepared to be cooperative.

When Marian and George visit the newspaper office, they explain that during the period of the shoot they will need to fasten a temporary sign over the permanent sign, which is carved in stone blocks on the outside of the building. The new sign Marian and George have designed, with the words "Erling Bugle" on it, will arrive with the rest of the shop-built scenery and props.

HOW ABOUT DUSTY ROSE, MRS. JONES?

The design crew visits Mrs. Jones's house, which will represent the exterior of the script character Patty's residence. The efficient production manager has arranged with Mrs. Jones to repaint her house exterior, which is now an unsuitable combination of colors for Patty's character. Marian explains that if she wishes, after the shoot is finished, they will repaint her house in the original colors. Mrs. Jones says that she will wait and see how she likes the new colors.

Marian also explains to her that they will have to make the outside of the house and yard look like winter. This will involve the placement of white fabric over the grass and covering it with plastic snow, as well as temporarily frosting the windows. They will also need to replace some leafed-out shrubbery with bare shrubbery, but will carefully remove the live plants and replant them when the shoot is over. This all sounds fine to Mrs. Jones, as she is getting a use fee for her property and a new paint job for her house.

PALMS IN DISGUISE

Marian and George scrutinize the business and street signs in the areas that will be seen on camera and photograph the ones that will need to be replaced or covered. A palm tree in front of the newspaper office will get a plastic shell around the trunk and blankets of leafy foliage around the fronds. After much measuring and photographing, Marian and George go back to the city to prepare finished construction drawings and get construction bids.

THE UNION

As this pilot episode will be made under union rules, the basic crew will be taken to the location and laborers and some assistants will be hired in Two Forks. If this town had its own union locals, the local office would provide all working personnel.

Two weeks later, when the chosen construction shop has begun building the sets, Marian and George pack their personal belongings and equipment for location. They take comfortable shoes, rain clothes, cameras, and basic drawing supplies. Living in a motel can be a dreary experience, but as the art staff spends the major part of the day and evening running around solving problems, they don't spend much time in those rooms with the bad paintings fastened to the walls.

WINTER AT 6:00 A.M.

Marian and George arrive in Two Forks two days before the first shoot day. The new signs and props have arrived by truck. They supervise the installation of the new signs, the repainting of Mrs. Jones's house, and the disguise of the palm tree in front of the newspaper office. They meet with the local helpers they will have and provide them with schedules for each of the shoot days, as well as meal vouchers redeemable at the local café.

The first shoot day, Marian meets George and their crew in the motel lobby at 6:00 A.M. The crew consists of a head prop person, assistant prop people, a truck driver, and four greenspeople who will prepare the planting at the Jones house. Marian goes over the day's schedule, which includes the first setup in front of the newspaper office, and after lunch, winter at the Jones house. Marian sends the greenspeople to the Jones house and she and George plus an assistant go to the newspaper exterior location.

The company is assembling on the street, and dipping into morning snacks prepared by the local café. Marian checks out the newspaper office sign and asks the video camera operator to take a look at the foliage hiding the palm tree. The operator lifts the camera up on the boom and Marian sees on the video monitor that a couple of palm fronds are showing in the shot. She asks one of her crew to go up on a ladder and fix the problem. George, meanwhile, sees that the cars hired to provide atmosphere have arrived and are waiting up the street for the assistant director to tell them what to do. He also notices that the gathered curtains they have placed on the inside of the newspaper office windows are bunched unevenly, so he asks an assistant to go in and straighten them.

By the time the tree dressing is finished, the cast and crew are ready to begin the first shot of the day. The action: The actor playing Patty parks in front of the newspaper office, gets out of a car, and enters the front door. The assistant director has coordinated the movements of the cars and the extras who walk down the sidewalk.

To deal with problems that may come up during the morning, George stays with the company and Marian goes to Mrs. Jones's house to supervise the winterizing project. Marian has the snow crew place more snow on the porch roof and spray-frost the side windows that will show in an angle shot. The crew has removed the leafed-out shrubbery and is beginning to place the bare shrubs.

The company arrives after lunch. By 5:00 P.M., when the light has changed too much to continue day scenes, everyone goes to dinner. They will reassemble later for night shooting in front of the house.

Marian and George spend much time sitting around waiting for the next camera setups during the day. As this is a video production, they can see the shots on a video monitor and can adjust set elements before the first take. Many motion picture companies use a video system that shows what the camera sees. Before this system was developed, only the camera operator could see the scene during the take.

After dinner and the night scenes are finished, Marian and George meet with their crew and go over the shooting schedule for tomorrow. George collects receipts from the crew for cash they have spent during the day. The production staff has a local bank account from which Marian can draw cash for out-of-pocket expenses. When Marian and George return to the motel, they balance out the cash and keep the receipts in their cash envelope.

The time is 10:30 P.M. The first location day is over and all went well, except for a noisy curiosity-seeking aircraft and a video recording problem. George and Marian retire to their respective rooms and set their alarms for 5:30 A.M. George turns on the local television news and there they are, turning summer to winter at Mrs. Jones's house. Two Forks is going to be famous!

BACK TO THE BIG CITY

When Marian and George view the footage at the postproduction facility, they hardly hear the dialogue. Their attention is focused on the work they did to alter the small-town environment, of course. They see that if the sign above the newspaper office entrance had been a couple of feet lower, it would have established itself better in the wide shot before the camera moved in to frame the front of the building. They also notice that the snow cover outside the house did not quite cover some grass down at the bottom of the frame, but as this was a night shot, a cast shadow covered the error. George is glad he took Polaroid pictures of the frost on the front windows of Mrs. Jones's house so they can duplicate the pattern on the inside of the stage sets. As a whole, however, they feel that their work was convincing to the camera.

Many art directors prefer to do location work, as it presents challenges and opportunities for improvisation, miles from nowhere. In the next chapter, we will see what an innovative art director can do with a commonplace design problem.

17

STAGING A TALK SHOW

The art director plays a major role in the presentation of a talk show. In the preceding example of the drama taking place in a small town in Iowa, the art director's job was to analyze the characters and their environments, to help create the mood of the drama, and to provide the physical requirements of the action. Other types of productions, however, offer few visual clues. What forms, colors, and textures will define the space, satisfy the practical requirements, and project a mood?

ANOTHER TALK SHOW?

Character definition is present here, as the producer tells us that the host is a warm, friendly person, and that the mood of the show is to be casual and relaxed. Right away, some obvious set solutions come to mind. How about the L-shaped couch, a coffee table with flowers, and bookcase walls with a fireplace? Well, that's always acceptable, but then we can do decorating jobs like that with our eyes shut if we drag out sets of drawings made three years ago. The producer, however, has had that one pulled on her before, and she is an expert cliché spotter.

Let's Hear It

The producer says, "I want to do something different. Just because the host has a friendly act going, I don't see that it's any reason to sit him behind a desk with a couch and coffee table. I want to see him in a simple set that will allow the cameras freedom of movement while they stay as close to invisible as possible." Our minds reel at the thought of having to do this. Here we thought this was going to be Talk Show A-1 and we could design it between coffee break and lunch.

This Is Going to Mean Real Work

"Tell me more," you say. "You want the cameras to move anywhere while they're invisible?" This producer talks as though she believes we are magicians instead of art directors.

She goes on. "What I am looking for is an arrangement that will allow the host and guest to be undistracted by the mechanics. I want them to be able to carry on an absorbing conversation without being distracted by studio activity. The viewer will be an eavesdropper. We're going to fade in on the conversation. The host is not going to turn to the camera and say, 'Hi! I'm so-and-so.'"

Well, here is a different idea. Maybe this will be fun. Might as well put the couch and coffee table back in storage. How are we going to hide all the studio apparatus and let the cameras float about wherever they will?

Let's Face It

To begin to solve the problem, we ask, What are the basic elements? Two seated people, the hidden cameras, and a background. When two people have a conversation, they usually face each other. If the camera sees them side by side, they will be in profile, which is tiresome. The cameras have to be able to get straight on at the two faces, but if they do that, are the cameras not going to see each other? Yes, they will, but if we set the two participants at a slight angle to each other, that will solve the problem.

THE GREAT CHAIR SEARCH

What kind of chair? The chair's design should prevent slouching and make the sitter appear to have good posture. The seat and back should be firmly upholstered so that the sitter does not sink in and appear to be part of the upholstery. The back of the chair should be invisible from the front so that the occupant does not appear to have grown wings. A useful type of chair is an upholstered dining armchair. Avoid the ones with high backs and choose a simple chair that fulfills the requirements but does not call attention to itself. Avoid swivel chairs unless they are specifically needed. Most professional performers can cope with swiveling, but when a nervous guest sits in a swivel chair, the viewer may get seasick watching the back-and-forth movement.

Seating on the Upper Platform Only

Because the four cameras to be used on this program are not going to be mounted on cranes or low dollies and cannot get down to the eye level of the host and guest, we will put the two chairs on a platform about eighteen inches high. This will allow the cameras a straight-on view of faces, rather than looking down on them. Place some steps, which can be integrated into the design of the platform, in convenient and safe places and make the risers (height) of each step no more than nine inches and the width no less than twelve inches. Cover the steps with nonskid material, which will prevent broken clavicles and lawsuits. When designing platforms on which people will be seated, allow a 4' x 4' space for each seated person. If the chairs are near the edges of the platform, fasten a strip of wood or metal to the edge to prevent chair legs from sliding off the platform.

DIFFERENT APPROACHES

Now that we have taken care of the chair and platform parts of the set, the most difficult problem faces us: the invisible cameras. How are we going to make the cameras invisible if they have to roam freely? One way would be to use a black cyclorama (background drapery) all the way around the stage and have the cameras work as far away as practical from the platform area. This means that the zoom lenses would have to be extended to a long focal length, which creates some perspective distortion, compressing the distance between two people, and flattening their faces. This is a minor problem, but a consideration. The cameras and camera operators may have to be draped in black fabric to make them blend into the black cyclorama. This approach, however, will leave our fascinating conversation sitting in a black void.

When the brain refuses to come up with another idea, go to a magazine rack and do some research, just as we did for the small town in Iowa. Architectural and home decoration magazines are full of *forms* that, if viewed as abstract shapes, can be developed into set pieces. The three basic shapes, circle, square, and triangle, are the basis of everything we see and can be put together in countless ways.

Scrim Shot

Aha, in an illustration we see some tall, sheer curtains hanging behind the front windows of a bank building. Because the light level outside the building is higher than that inside the building, the curtains are opaque from the outside and transparent from the inside of the building.

Aping the bank building drapery, we could hang a stretched scrim (gauze curtain) from the grid to the stage floor, eight feet or more out from the stage walls, going around three sides of the stage. If the scrim is a light color, it will reflect light striking it and hide the cameras working behind it. Because the lenses will be looking through gauze, the pictures will have a soft, diffused look, which might be objectionable. This approach will require testing to see if it will work.

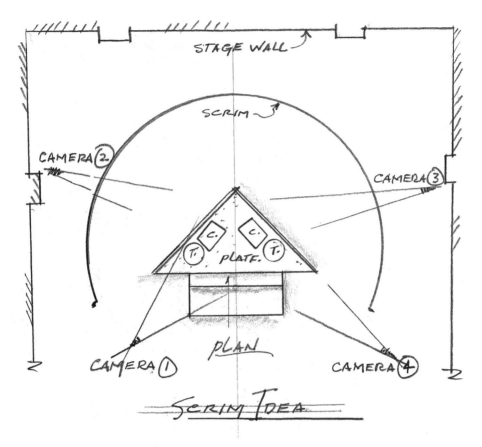

Quick, Draw the Blinds!

Another magazine picture shows some tall vertical sun-control vanes out-side the windows. When viewed from one angle, the group of vanes appears to be a solid wall, but when seen from another angle, the spaces between the panels reveal what is behind them. We could construct some 4-foot-wide vertical vanes, similar to those in the picture, that would hide the cameras and operators when seen from most angles, yet would allow the lenses a clear field to shoot the central area from other angles. A consultation with the director is in order here before proceeding with this idea, as the director will have to work with this set and its built-in advantages and disadvantages. Here is an opportunity to build a simple model of the set that can be viewed at eye level to reveal possible angles.

THE IDEAL SOLUTION

Good ideas can come from unexpected places. None of us has a bottomless supply of visual images, but if we learn to look at the images surrounding us with a fresh eye, we can apply them to our design work.

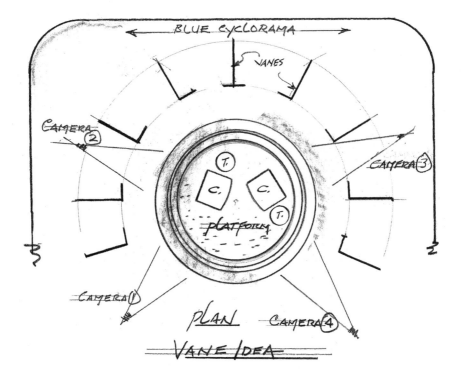

Be Imaginative

It's always a pleasure to work with producers and directors who are not willing to settle for obvious solutions, but we must be ready to accept failure as well. If you are interested in helping the producer and director come up with innovative solutions to their staging problems, you will find that they are usually willing to listen to an idea that is out of the ordinary. If the idea does not work, you can add it to your list of nonworking but interesting solutions. Perhaps constantly improving technology will allow you to drag the idea out of the drawer in the future.

Innovative solutions can be applied to other forms of programming as well. In the next chapter we will see how the art director works out several solutions to a news set and what the reception is.

STAGING A
NEWS BROADCAST

News broadcasting is a major source of income for most television stations in the United States and receives a large share of management's attention. In the past, news broadcasting played a minor role because viewers wanted to be entertained rather than informed. This is still the case. Ratings rose when broadcasters increased the entertainment values in news and introduced attractive news-reading personalities. Appearance and style became important. As audience ratings increased, so did the amount of money television could charge for commercial time.

The length of the broadcasts increased to allow more time for entertainment and production values. Technological advances changed the nature of news presentations. Not long after the first television pictures flickered into our living rooms, news events were covered by sending huge trucks full of equipment to an event, bringing it into our homes while it was happening. Film cameras were used to record events that we saw with the delay of a few hours. The development of magnetic recording techniques allowed broadcasters to record and play back instantly, if necessary, and released broadcasters from the film laboratory delay.

WHAT DOES THIS HAVE TO DO WITH ART DIRECTION?

Art directors are involved with the presentation of news broadcasts. Broadcasters strive to outdo each other with the authority, entertainment values, and exciting look of their news services. The care a designer puts into the set affects the quality of the broadcast.

Broadcasters place much emphasis on the appearance of the people who talk to the cameras as well as the environment in which they are seen. The audience has the impression that their favorite performers rush around all day and night gathering news to share. The reality is that the many people who are invisible to the home audience do most of the gathering and rushing. Newsroom presentations require the art director to create an authentic-looking, workable environment for the news-gathering and on-camera staff. The designer also must understand the requirements of graphic effects to provide the necessary elements in the set.

MAKE IT LOOK LIKE A NEWSROOM!

Let's look in on a typical production meeting at which a new news presentation is born. The management of WXXX has decided to abandon their traditional format, three people seated at a curved desk in front of a photomural. WXXX is going to jump on the bandwagon and do a newsroom-format program two hours long that will sweep the ratings in Midland City, Illinois.

Present at the meeting are the news director, program director, station manager, production manager, art director, graphics supervisor, technical director, facilities manager, assorted assistants, and twenty personalized coffee cups.

After the usual preliminary greetings and chit-chat with which all meetings begin, the station manager says, "I have called this meeting to get the ball rolling on the new secret news show that you all know about. We've been concerned about the success of the newsroom format over at Channel 8 and in other markets around the country. We're not going to be left behind . . . (etc., etc.). Now our illustrious news director is going to tell you about this exciting new project." (Has anyone heard of a *dull* new project?)

John, the news director, starts in. Everyone takes notes. He says the new show will be two hours long, have a newsroom format, and that the news staff will be seen on camera doing what will appear to be their regular jobs. We hear a lot of brave talk about how terrific it will be and how there will be some new mobile units that will solve all the news-gathering problems. In other words, it's going to be a *new look*!

Stifle That Groan

These words rouse Harold, the art director, from his lethargy. New Looks always mean they will want a set that looks completely different in two weeks and will cause viewers to become so excited they will not think of switching over to the dreaded Channel 8. "What kind of a look do you want?" Harold asks.

"We want the viewers to feel the excitement of a real newsroom where things are happening—that they are right in the middle of it!" the news director says. Harold wonders how exciting he can make a couple of rows of people typing.

"When is all this supposed to go on the air?" Harold asks.

"We're shooting for September eighth," Mr. Station Manager replies.

A hush falls over the room. Taking a grip on his coffee cup, Harold says, "That gives me a whole three weeks, then. I don't see how I can design and build a whole new newsroom by then." All eyes turn to the news director.

He says, "Don't worry. All we have to do is move the cameras into the old newsroom and put in some lights."

DETERMINING THE REQUIREMENTS

Harold asks some more questions and returns to his cubicle to begin organizing this new challenge. Setting aside the problems posed by the low ceiling in the existing newsroom, with its attendant lighting difficulties, Harold makes a list of the requirements outlined at the meeting.

Anchor desk with four positions
Chromakey effect (blue or green area for inserting electronic graphics)
Program title and channel number in every shot
Clocks showing world time
Map of the world
Map of the state
Bank of TV screens

Measuring the Room

Harold's first job is to record the general dimensions of the room, including the height of the ceiling, changes in floor level, width and height of the doors, and jogs in the walls. He also measures and counts the desks, knowing that for camera purposes some of them will have to be moved. He also takes note of the kinds of electrical and communication outlets that will be a factor in the desk arrangement.

Back to the Drawing Board

Armed with these numbers, Harold begins to sketch out some ideas on pieces of tracing paper. He starts with some obvious solutions, such as just painting the walls and putting in an anchor desk or moving the newsroom to a broadcasting studio, but no, he is stuck with the requirements as outlined in the meeting.

Scale It Up

To be sure that the new set will fit into the existing room, Harold makes a plan view scale drawing of the room and makes scale cardboard shapes of the working desks and other necessary objects. By trying different arrangements of the desk shapes, he can get a clearer idea of the spaces. When he has a preliminary arrangement, he takes the time to make a simple scale model of the room. Now the forms are even more clear and he can hold the model up at eye level and see what the camera angles can be and where changes can be made.

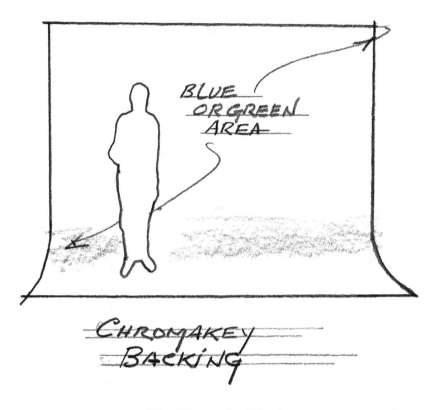

CHROMAKEY BACKING

The Key to the Weather

The next item is the Chromakey area for the weather person. The news director has decided to use the new computer graphics system in combination with the Chromakey effect. Chromakey is an electronic system that inserts a picture wherever the camera sees a selected color. The most useful colors are saturated blue or green because they are far away in the spectrum from flesh tones. If you were to use pink, for example, as the background color, the system would read the pinkish flesh tones of the person standing in front of the pink background and the face and hands would disappear. Also, bright blue and green are not popular apparel colors and would not be likely to interfere with the electronic processing.

The Number and the Title

The next item on Harold's list is channel number and program title in every shot. At this point in the design process, he has only a rough idea of the camera angles and can only estimate where the logos should go, based on his squint at the model at eye level. Any critical placement of objects such as logos should be done when the camera angles are pretty well established. Harold decides to make some logos of different sizes and experiment with the director's assistance.

Clutter Everywhere

Looking at the newsroom as it exists, Harold sees that it is a visual mess, has no central area, and no color identity. The room serves its purpose as a utilitarian space where work is done, but it will look incoherent and confusing on camera. Armed with the information obtained with measuring tape and the model, he decides to make a central area toward the end of the room where the cameras will be. This area will be elevated eighteen inches above floor level to get the seated, on-camera people's eyes looking directly into the camera. This area will be the anchor-desk area, and the background will be feverish news-gathering activity taking place on the main floor level. The back wall can display the clocks and banks of TV screens, as well as the program title and channel number. Harold decides to create a couple of set walls for the world map and state map. The director and Harold can experiment on camera to see where the best locations will be for these walls.

This Is Creative?

While the group of elements Harold has assembled is a standard one, they will communicate that this is a news-gathering area full of busy people. His goal has been to get a general idea of the spaces, what the arrangement can be, and what the cameras will see. At this point, Harold is in control of the visual situation, as the producer and director are planning the content and organization of the program presentation. They probably do not have specific ideas of the wall colors and details and depend on Harold to make a presentation.

Although Harold has made some rough plans and sketches, he makes another scale drawing of the newsroom. He decides to use 1/4" = 1' for the floor plan and 1/2" = 1' for the elevation drawings. As the people to whom he will show the drawings are not accustomed to looking at scale plans and probably will not understand them, he makes some sketches of what the camera will see from different angles, including scale human-figure outlines for size reference.

HAROLD IS GOING TO SCARE THEM

During the design process, he works up three ideas for the newsroom and decides to provide some choices. He makes presentation sketches of three ideas for consideration:

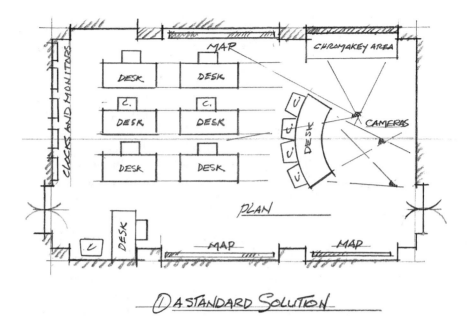

① A STANDARD SOLUTION

1. *A standard solution.* Following the news director's requirements, Harold places a four-person anchor desk in the foreground, a big station logo and Chromakey green area to the left, and a row of clocks on the wall above. The walls are textured beige.
2. *A different arrangement of the same idea.* This version of the set has some colored panels, a comfortable-looking interview area at the

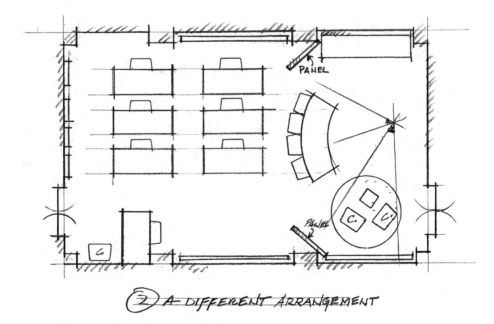

② A DIFFERENT ARRANGEMENT

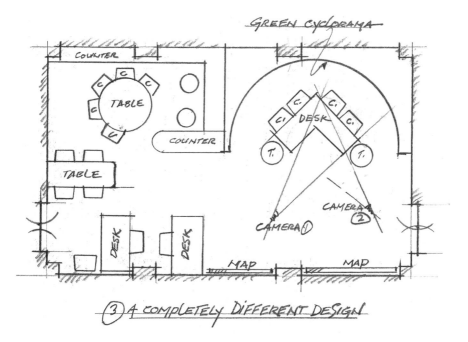

③ A COMPLETELY DIFFERENT DESIGN

side of the desk, and chrome trim around the walls. Everything else is the same.

3. *A completely different design that will possibly frighten everyone.* This scary idea has no conventional walls, but a 180-degree green cyclorama, which is used to show colorful computer-stored news graphics and videotape behind the news talent, who sit in comfortable chairs on a raised platform. A curved transparent surface in front of them holds papers and a transparent globe. Their legs show.

The three choices will give the staff a chance to show their true colors. Mr. Cautious will go for set No. 1 and possibly set No. 2 if he feels daring. Mr. Middle-of-the-Road will not say anything until he hears the station manager's opinion. Ms. Courageous will go for No. 3, whatever may happen.

What's the Decision?

When creating projects such as news presentations that are financially important to a television operation, the management is cautious with a never-before-tried solution. After hours of soul-searching and argument and mind-changing, the middle-of-the-road approach was selected. Harold files Design No. 3 for another day.

In the next chapter, we will see what an art director can do to present a lot of visual information in a short period of time. Television commercials are usually produced very quickly and are a good test of an art director's skill.

19

DESIGNING A COMMERCIAL

Besides giving us the chance to dash to the refrigerator for a snack, television commercials support the programming that keeps us on the couch in the first place.

The objective of a television commercial is to sell a product, of course. By interviewing consumers and by analyzing sales and demographic data, advertising agencies create commercials that they believe will cause the consumer, consciously or unconsciously, to buy one product instead of another. The consumer's choice may not have any bearing on the intrinsic worth of the product but can simply be an unconscious response to the atmosphere in which the product is presented. The art director, then, as a participant in the creation of the environment, helps sell a product.

What is the difference between an advertising agency art director and a video or film art director? The agency art director works with the agency creative director in creating the storyboard and general visual concept for the commercial. The *storyboard* is a series of drawings in panels much like

STORYBOARD PANELS

a comic strip layout that shows the progressive action with the dialogue beneath each picture. The video or film art director, working from the storyboard and script, makes the general idea concrete by designing the set or sets as outlined in the script and storyboard. The video or film art director is usually hired by the production house with the approval of the advertising agency. Many art directors specialize in the design of commercials.

COMMERCIAL PRODUCTION PERSONNEL

Client whose product is advertised
Advertising agency that creates the commercial idea
    Agency producer
    Creative director
    Copy writer
    Agency art director

Production house
    Director
    Art director
    Set decorator
    Food stylist
    Director of photography (DP)
    Stage facility
    Postproduction services

DEALING WITH CHOICES

The art director who designs the sets works with the three groups of people: client, agency, and production house. Differences of opinion occur that affect the art director's work. Someone may not like the wallpaper, another the set dressing, or another the paint color. The producer has the final say as far as the art director is concerned, and may have to work out compromises with the different factions. This is another time when the art director has to be diplomatic.

DAILY LABOR

The set art director is usually hired to work on a daily basis rather than under a contract arrangement. The amount of time available for the art director to design and assemble the elements of the job is short in most cases, frequently just three or four days. The client, of course, wants to know exactly what the sets are going to look like, so an art director's ability to prepare accurate sketches is important. An 8 1/2" x 11" copy of the original set sketch should be provided as well, as this size can be faxed and included with scripts.

LABELING AND FOOD

Usually the advertising agency prepares camera-ready labels and packaging for the products, as regular labels may not photograph clearly. Larger production centers use art services that specialize in product labels for video and film, but frequently the art director handles this part of the job as well, using Photostats, typesetting, laser copying, and airbrush. If the commercial needs food preparation, the agency or production house will hire a food stylist who will attractively cook and prepare the necessary dishes.

SKETCHES AND PLANS

The set art director prepares sketches and construction drawings and submits them to several construction shops for competitive bids, unless the production house has made other arrangements. Construction drawings with specific detailed information are very useful in this case, as shops will increase their bids to cover unknown labor and materials if they do not know exactly what is required. Sometimes there is not time to provide detailed construction drawings and the set may be built from a sketch with dimensions indicated on the sketch.

MONEY MATTERS

Some art directors specializing in commercials contract for their services for a flat fee, including construction costs, helpers, and props. This is OK if you are experienced and know exactly what you are doing, but as a rule, it is better to have the production house, producer, or agency handle all the contracts, payments, and out-of-pocket costs. Never spend your own money, as it is frequently difficult to get it back again. A viable company will give the art director cash for small items, for which you must account with receipts after the production is finished.

HERE'S THE SCRIPT

Now that the ground rules are entrenched in your mind, read the script that has been delivered by special messenger.

HUFFNAGEL, TWITCHELL & BURNS ADVERTISING
1201 ANONYMOUS PARKWAY
PONCA CITY, CA 90000
(213) 456-7890

30-SECOND TELEVISION SPOT #345
CLIENT: ACME DETERGENTS
PRODUCT: JIFFY CLEANER

CREATIVE DIRECTOR: DAWN DAILY
ART DIRECTOR: PAT TERRIFIC

SETTING: High-rise condo in Midtown, U.S.A., kitchen.
TIME: 6:30 P.M., weekday, winter.
CU HARASSED SWEATY FACE OF BRUCE BUMMER,
HOUSEHUSBAND OF FLEUR EAGER-BUMMER, 30-SOME-
THING INVESTMENT ANALYST

CAMERA PULLS BACK, REVEALING BRUCE SCRUBBING
THE SINK BASEBOARD WITH STEEL WOOL.

FLEUR ENTERS, CARRYING A POWER BRIEFCASE. SHE
SLAMS THE CASE DOWN ON THE BREAKFAST BAR.

                    FLEUR
What <u>are</u> you doing, Bruce?

BRUCE STANDS UP INTO FRAME—2 SHOT

                    BRUCE
Just trying to get that scuff mark off the baseboard,
that's all. This has been some day! First, the couch didn't
come from Bloomie's.... Then, Roger called and talked for
an hour and a half, and then....

                    FLEUR
Never mind. I've got just the thing.

CUT TO: CU FLEUR TAKES SPRAY BOTTLE OF JIFFY
CLEANER OUT OF HER BRIEFCASE.

JIFFY will get rid of that scuff in a jiffy and won't leave a
stain!

BRUCE

You think of everything, honey. Why don't you slip into something more comfortable and I'll whip up some pasta.

BRUCE'S HAND CARESSES FLEUR'S OVER THE BOTTLE OF JIFFY CLEANSER.

MUSIC: ROMANTIC VIOLINS

FLEUR

Never mind the pasta, honey. Just take care of the baseboard.

LAP DISSOLVE TO: MOON RISING BEHIND SKYSCRAPERS.

MUSIC RISES AND ENDS.

THE BASIC SET

Commercials have to present a lot of information in a short period of time. Each set element contributes to the viewer's perception of the characters, their environment, and above all, the product being presented. In some

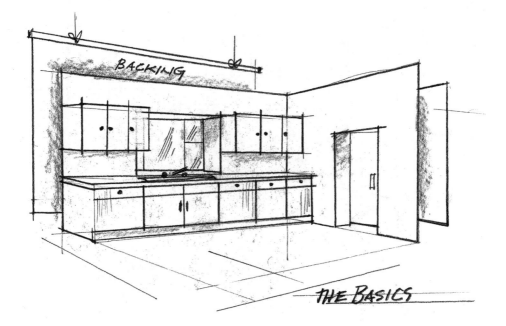

cases the product is the atmosphere created by the setting, communicating elegance, speed, efficiency, or other salable attributes.

Remember that to give the impression of a high-rise condominium building, you need not build the entire building with a complete four-walled kitchen. One of the art director's jobs is to select the elements that give the impression required by the script.

Two walls set at an angle to each other will be a start. One wall needs a door through which Fleur can enter. The other wall can have a window, kitchen sink, and cabinets.

AN IMPROVED SET

Let's add some visual interest to this simple set. Put the sink in a freestanding island with a cooktop and work surface. Even better, make the island an L-shaped unit. This will be more exciting. The previous sink-below-the-window approach would have worked but would not have given the impression that Fleur and Bruce are upscale people. Also, we now have given the director many opportunities for delicious three-dimensional compositions and many choices of camera angles.

Turning our attention to the former sink wall, it can now hold the window through which we see the moon and skyscrapers and can also hold

IMPROVED KITCHEN

cabinets, refrigerator, counter, and ovens, all custom-built into the wall, of course.

Remember that when Fleur opens the kitchen door, the camera will have to see something outside the door besides a napping stagehand. Assuming she is coming in the back door of the condominium, design a portion of the condominium-complex hallway to be seen when she opens the door. Another opening will be the window, through which we need to see a city-at-night vista and the moon. A backlit translucent backing of the same will serve the purpose. If the scene on the backing shows the city view from ground level, roll up the bottom of the backing on its batten so that the perspective becomes that seen from a high building.

The script calls for Fleur to slam her briefcase on the breakfast bar. If we make this bar a freestanding movable breakfast bar, the director can place it wherever the action demands. Movable pieces of scenery (called wild units) provide flexibility when composing shots.

Pay close attention to the crucial area where Bruce is trying to scrub off the scuff mark. See that the carpenters pay meticulous attention to the finish of the baseboard. The advertising agency people will scrutinize this area because this is where their stain-remover product will work its magic. They may hire an expert technician to apply just the right mark that can be easily, but honestly, removed.

What about color? Fleur and Bruce, trendy couple that they are, would probably have the very latest color or no color in their kitchen: possibly charcoal countertops with just a little chrome trim, and a no-nonsense stainless steel restaurant range or cook top.

When choosing the set dressing, again keep your knowledge of the characters in mind. Bruce, successful househusband that he is, would hardly have a set of kitchen canisters shaped like teddy bears, would he?

When the set is up, dressed, and the shoot day arrives, keep calm. People will drift onto the stage and begin making comments. Be flexible and be prepared to change some things such as the color of the door, the position of the sink, or any other alteration that satisfies someone's need to suggest changes. After all, you know that this is a beautiful set and will make an enhancing addition to your sample reel.

In the preceding chapters, we have seen examples of design and production successes as well as problems. The only way to get some real-life experience is to begin working in the art direction profession. Turn to the next chapter for some helpful tips.

20

WHERE AND HOW TO LOOK FOR WORK

Where can you start? Let's look at some allied fields that need people with the skills to assemble two- and three-dimensional objects in a practical and pleasing way and proceed from those to your goal as an art director.

HOW TO GET YOUR FOOT IN THE DOOR

If you attend a college or university that has a television and/or film department, present yourself at the doorstep. Over one thousand colleges and universities offer courses in film and video and many have production facilities. Even though you may be an art student or in some other area of the school, see if the film and video department needs assistance with sets, lighting, or other aspects of production. Learn as much as you can about your own job as well as lighting, sound, camera, writing, and carpentry. Some art and architectural students work out arrangements between departments so that projects that involve both academic areas can be devised.

Windows and Interiors

A department store display department is an excellent place to gain experience in three-dimensional design. The merchandise a store sells is as important in its presentation as the actors in a drama. In the same way that the sets should not overwhelm the actors, the environment for a department store mannequin or product should not dominate the merchandise. You can gain valuable experience in presentation, which will be an important part of creating successful television or film settings.

Come On Now, Smile!

Another entry point can be through commercial photography. Many still photographers employ stylists who collect props for settings. In some cases, the stylist scouts locations for the photographer and will make alterations and additions. Stylists usually find the clothing and accessories for the models as well as designing and dressing the setting. Photographers work for newspapers, advertising agencies, magazines, educational videos, and corporate training films and videos.

You're Getting Closer

Small theater groups are eager to have talented people help with scenic work, especially if they show up when it's time to work. As their budgets are small, little theater set design requires much improvisation from the designer, a useful skill no matter how large the budget.

Are You Connected?

Most communities are served by cable television systems that offer the use of their facilities to citizens who wish to put on their own programs for transmission over the local system. In many areas, cable operators offer free instruction to anyone who is willing to attend a few classes covering technical operation of the equipment. Public-access programming is one of the most interesting forms of television and is accessible in most communities.

GETTING YOUR ACT TOGETHER

When you go to the big city to seek your fortune, you will discover many other people there who are trying to do the same thing. To help you get a head start, here are some suggestions.

Prepare a simple one-page résumé listing your name, address, phone number, and experience. Have some business cards to leave. Be sure the phone number you give is served by an answering machine or someone who is there to answer calls.

The Mechanics

Use a weatherproof, zipper portfolio and mount your photographs and drawings neatly on matching-size clean mat boards or inside clear acetate pages. Fold blueprints to a manageable size. Rolled prints are difficult to hold open for viewing. If you have done film or tape, prepare a sample reel to show. Portfolio cases that allow the removal of pages work well, as you can edit your presentation to suit the needs of the person you will see. Don't talk your way through each page. Let the person to whom you show your work make the comments and ask the questions.

GETTING INTERVIEWS

Once you've prepared a great portfolio and have résumés and cards printed, how do you find the job opportunities? First come the telephone book yellow pages, with listings under film producers, film production companies, television stations, film commercial producers, advertising agencies, and commercial photographers. Use the telephone and ask to speak to whomever is in charge of production. Make an appointment if he or she is willing or mail a résumé. Follow up on interviews and mailed résumés by telephoning in a few weeks, but don't irritate a prospective employer with too many inquiries.

Research the needs of the company. A motion picture supervising art director doesn't necessarily want to see examples of jewelry design. Don't show too many samples. Remember that the prospective employer is probably very busy and can perceive your talents from about a dozen examples of your work.

OPPORTUNITIES IN VIDEO DESIGN

When you have some experience in entry-level positions and some impressive samples of your work, where do you look for a television job?

Local Television

A small station in a local market is a good place to start. As the designer has to do a little bit of everything in these situations, the beginner has a chance to focus interests and learn what set and graphic design require on a daily basis.

Some of these television stations are affiliated with a network and some are independent. Affiliated stations carry a contracted amount of network programming, which allows the network exposure for their commercial clients and allows the local affiliate to carry network programming that attracts viewers. Television networks are allowed to own television broadcasting stations, which are usually in major cities. The design policies of these owned stations usually follow the policy of the network. Independent stations have no network affiliation and buy syndicated programming from various producers and syndicators. A designer usually has more freedom at an independent station and can create design programs without outside design-policy interference.

Network Television

The commercial television networks have major production facilities in New York and Los Angeles. They produce their own programming as well as buy some from independent producers. In the past, when the networks produced much more of their own programming, they maintained larger staffs of art directors and graphic designers than they do now.

Independent Producers

Many art directors are employed by individual producers, who sell their product to networks. Art directors commonly work on a freelance basis for these producers. Most of the television series are produced by independents. The producer may get money from a network to produce a pilot (sample program). If the program has possibilities as a series, the producer is given a contract to produce a group of episodes.

Corporate Video

Some large corporations maintain film and video production staffs that produce information videos. These programs present training, technical, news, and employee relations material. Outside production companies are contracted for the bulk of the work. Presentation of technical information uses graphic art for diagrams, graphs, and flow charts as well as stage settings and location work. A corporate public relations office may give the aspiring designer a list of producers who produce videos and films for them. However, the telephone classified directory is also a good bet, listing corporate video producers.

MOTION PICTURE OPPORTUNITIES

Many designers move from video to the motion picture world, where the pay is better and the productions are generally more interesting. Many motion picture studios no longer have functioning art departments because independent producers hire their own production staffs. A large production company may have a supervising art director who hires art directors and set designers to work on specific productions. They may work on the lot where the production facilities are located. The production designer who works on a film assembles the design staff.

The Union

As in many other areas of work, such as manufacturing and trades, technicians and artists in the early days of motion picture production found it necessary to band together to improve their working conditions and economic positions.

Producers who have signed union contracts are required to hire union members as long as they are available. The advantage of belonging to a union is that the worker is guaranteed certain working conditions and wages. This presents a problem for the beginner, as you can't get into the union until you work a union production and you can't work a union production until you are a union member. However, an art director or set designer who is working a nonunion production that "goes union" during production becomes eligible for union membership at that point. The inductee then pays an initiation fee and quarterly dues.

Nonunion Productions

Many production designers, art directors, and set designers start out on nonunion productions and many continue along this path. The individual art director then negotiates salary, working conditions, and length of employment. A few agents represent successful art directors and negotiate salary and working conditions for them.

Other States

Now that location filming has become popular, every state and the larger cities have film offices that are responsible for attracting film companies as well as maintaining lists of available personnel and services. These film offices are information centers for upcoming activity, and art directors are wise to be listed with them.

Networking

The crew with which you work on a production is a good source of job information and referral. Exchange cards during this "one big happy family" situation. Personal recommendation by others with whom you have worked is a great source of work. Trade magazines and newspapers contain valuable information on productions in the planning stages as well as employment opportunities in the classified pages.

INDEX